Understanding the Human Mind

The Mystery of Hypnosis

Jason Browne

© Copyright 2021 - All rights reserved.

The content contained within this book may not be reproduced, duplicated or transmitted without direct written permission from the author or the publisher.

Under no circumstances will any blame or legal responsibility be held against the publisher, or author, for any damages, reparation, or monetary loss due to the information contained within this book, either directly or indirectly.

Legal Notice:

This book is copyright protected. It is only for personal use. You cannot amend, distribute, sell, use, quote or paraphrase any part, or the content within this book, without the consent of the author or publisher.

Disclaimer Notice:

Please note the information contained within this document is for educational and entertainment purposes only. All effort has been executed to present accurate, up to date, reliable, complete information. No warranties of any kind are declared or implied. Readers acknowledge that the author is not engaged in the rendering of legal, financial, medical or professional advice. The content within this book has been derived from various sources. Please consult a licensed professional before attempting any techniques outlined in this book.

By reading this document, the reader agrees that under no circumstances is the author responsible for any losses, direct or indirect, that are incurred as a result of the use of the information contained within this document, including, but not limited to, errors, omissions, or inaccuracies.

Table of Contents

INTRODUCTION 1

CHAPTER 1: AN OVERVIEW ON THE HISTORY OF HYPNOSIS ... 9

PREHISTORIC ROOTS 9
SCIENTIFIC HISTORY 13
THRIVING MOMENTUM 17

CHAPTER 2: HOW HYPNOSIS HAS EVOLVED OVER TIME 25

SURPRISING PRACTICES 26
PERIODIC APPLICATIONS 29
MODERN EXPANSION 34

CHAPTER 3: DEFINING HYPNOSIS 39

THE FACE OF HYPNOSIS 39
Myth 1: Hypnosis Induces a Different State of Mind or Consciousness 41
Myth 2: Hypnosis and Meditation Must Be One of the Same 43
Myth 3: Too Few People Are Genuinely Suggestible 45
Myth 4: It's All a Bunch of Pretentious Play 48
Myth 5: Hypnosis Doesn't Change Anything on a Physical or Chemical Level 49
Other Common Myths 51

CHAPTER 4: WHY AND HOW SELF-HYPNOSIS WORKS 55

SELF-HYPNOSIS EXPLAINED 56
Tips for Recording 59
THE BRAIN UNDER HYPNOSIS 62

CHAPTER 5: BEGINNER'S GUIDE TO INDUCTION 71

INDUCTION BASICS 71

- Rapid Inductions 77
- Conversational Inductions 80
- Progressive Inductions 82
- Fixation Inductions 85

CHAPTER 6: HYPNOSIS AS A THERAPEUTIC PRACTICE 89

- Basic Improvements 90
- Mental Health Potentials 92
- Physical Health Opportunities 96

CHAPTER 7: NEURO-LINGUISTIC PROGRAMMING (NLP) 103

- NLP Explained 104
- What to Expect 109
- Favorite Techniques 114

CHAPTER 8: OTHER MODERN METHODS OF HYPNOSIS 119

- Suggestion Hypnosis 120
- Regression Hypnotherapy 122
- Primers 126
- Ericksonian Hypnotherapy 128
- Self-Hypnosis 131

CONCLUSION 137

REFERENCES 143

Introduction

Robertson Davies once said, "The eye sees only what the mind is prepared to comprehend." If anything could explain the mystery of hypnosis in one sentence, it would be just that. Whether you want to improve your scripts, or you're looking at starting a hypnotherapy habit but don't know what it entails, unraveling the mysteries behind a vastly misunderstood technique as old as the Egyptian pharaohs is a good starting point. The veil that prevents you from reaping the benefits from a scientifically proven practice is mostly designed by unreliable information, misconceptions, and a lack of knowing how to start your hypnosis journey. Maybe you've tried hypnosis before, and it didn't have the effects you hoped for. Anyone who has learned to master their minds, thoughts, goals, and emotions through this invaluable practice will tell you that you've just been exposed to the wrong type of information.

The internet is a wonderful place we can all gather information from, but there's no real way of knowing whether we read facts or fiction. One website tells you about a hypnotic induction that puts you in a sleep state, and another one claims to have all the secrets to making your self-hypnosis journey as easy as pie. In contradiction, you also read content on a website that explains how only some people can be hypnotized. The statistics aren't in your favor, so you close the web page before you even read the full article. Let's not mention that you also don't worry about cross-referencing the sources to see if the information is reliable or not. Hypnosis poses a cloud of mystery because of the internet. Sadly, too many pages are written by people who know nothing about it. Additionally, you have a few people claiming to be able to hypnotize someone to do things against their will.

Your skepticism crosses the border to fear as you wonder what you'll be asked to do under hypnosis. Suddenly, images of Las Vegas come to mind where people are clucking like chickens on stage. You may even recall a show where the hypnotist suggested that the volunteer call their girlfriend and break it off with her. Beyond the stage performances and people claiming to manipulate others with hypnotic trances, you also start thinking about the scary images of snakes and shadow dancing in some weird movie you watched. To make your mystery fall into the depth of misconception, you have a bad experience with a hypnotherapist. You don't believe the session did you any good, and you felt uncomfortable. The hypnotherapist was the icing on the cake that made you question what hypnosis really is and isn't.

It's good to want to know more about a technique used all over the world today, but it's a terrible idea to rely on the opposing information you're finding from unreliable sources. At the end of the day, you'll be worsening your situation instead of improving your life, health, and goal achievements. The only way anyone can grab what they want by the horns and make it theirs is to control the core principle behind it, which starts in the human mind. Everything in your world is controlled by your mind. Your thoughts, actions, emotions, perceptions, and achievements depend on how much control you possess over your neurological components. Hypnosis is not some scary stage performance or dark form of manipulation. Some people may use it for untoward reasons, but most people successfully find a type of hypnosis that works wonders for them and their personal needs.

Hypnosis, in its many modern forms, is a technique used to grab those horns and take charge. Even better, it's not what you think. Most people think hypnosis is a way for others to take control of your mind, and some people believe you fall asleep, but both statements are incorrect. You also don't lose the ability to choose what you need. In most cases, the reasons people fail with hypnosis are that they tried it wrong, had the wrong intentions, or never learned about the facts behind the practice. Comprehensive research conducted by Binghamton University was published in *Pseudoscience* (Lynn et al., 2018). The researchers looked at various facts and myths surrounding hypnosis, and they clarified what has been scientifically proven. For one, hypnosis is a credible form of therapy because neurological and psychological changes have been noted. Clinical hypnosis and stage performances are also two entirely different concepts.

Additionally, the research by Binghamton University found that people don't enter a sleep-like state or become robotic, and they maintain their control over their minds throughout the sessions provided by clinical hypnotherapists. Further myths were busted, and knowing the facts around genuine hypnosis used for medical and psychological purposes can help you practice the type that benefits you the most, but that's an unraveled mystery for the coming pages. What you'll find when you journey through fact-based evidence, history, and simple techniques to promote better hypnosis in clinical and personal settings is that you'll finally establish the right relationship with a technique that could open new doors for you, and you'll know just how effective it is. Some people wrongly believe that hypnosis was some stage performance at first, but this use of it was influenced by science and ancient history.

The history itself is eye-opening, and it can explain better how modern hypnosis came about. You'll learn how hypnosis changed over time as new interests peaked in some names we commonly hear in science. Sigmund Freud was but one man we famously know for other theories in behavioral sciences, but he was not the founding father of modern hypnosis. You'll also find out what really happens when you experience a hypnotic state, and we'll blow all the myths out of the water. One of the greatest lessons you'll learn from research is that hypnosis is a cognitive skill. It's something you can possess, improve, and apply to any changes you want in your life. You'll also understand what happens in the brain when you practice hypnosis, and you'll delve into a few secrets the brain unfolds to make the technique work in your favor, even if you're new to hypnosis.

Modern hypnosis also allows you to experiment with various types of induction and deepening because little do many people know that anyone with the right tools can succeed in hypnotherapy. Suggestibility is another misunderstood concept that you'll clarify. Numerous inductions can be used, depending on what makes you fall into the relaxed state you need to successfully apply strong suggestions. From progressive to conversational induction, you may even learn how to bring someone else into a relaxed state of mind with some practice. Some people are so good with conversational suggestions that they can hypnotize someone as soon as they walk through the door. This doesn't give them boundless control over that person's mind, but they can encourage a hypnotic state simply by having three tools. These tools can also help you use some simple techniques on other people if you wish, but that's saved for dark hypnosis.

The point of learning the three tools and the secrets to making hypnosis successful is to practice self-hypnosis for your ultimate and ever-changing needs. You'll also learn about the immense benefits you can enjoy professionally, mentally, physically, and emotionally if you find the right hypnotherapy type. Additionally, hypnosis is not some vague idea in professional terms anymore. Today, there are six popular and modern types used, and you'll know what to expect from each one. From neuro-linguistic programming to Ericksonian hypnotherapy and self-hypnosis, knowing your options means you have a greater chance of success. Otherwise, if you're already practicing self-hypnosis but want to improve your scripts, you'll find many simple secrets hidden among these pages. Hypnosis isn't a mystery once you find your holy grail and use proven techniques to reinforce it.

I've been studying hypnosis for five years now, and I can happily say that I've helped hundreds of people achieve the results they wanted. Not everyone responds to hypnosis the same way, but finding those unique patterns is what makes the journey exciting. Even I must change my patterns from time to time so I can keep up with the inevitable changes in my life. However, I can't begin to express the magnitude of what hypnosis has done for me. The ability to control my thoughts and actions outweighs the time it took me to master my practice. Watching the people I've helped grow and flourish as they learned to master their minds has also motivated me to reach out to more people.

I've always had this ingrained fascination with the human mind, and maybe that's what brought you to the door of hypnotic curiosity, but I guarantee you one thing; hypnosis will not disappoint you if you're fascinated by the workings and ultimate potential of the human mind. Whether you're a beginner who wants to get into the art of mind mastery, or you have prior experience with hypnosis and want to expand your potential, you're one page away from starting your journey. Welcome to the incredible world of hypnosis.

Step into the first chapter whenever you're feeling amped.

Chapter 1:

An Overview on the History of Hypnosis

Hypnotism is much older than people believe, well, some form of it anyway. The history paints a colorful picture of who practiced the first types of hypnotism. The motivation behind the practice changed over time, but a few varying techniques have set the stage for what we know today. From ancient practices as old as sorcery and early medicine to names we hear often in other fields in modern times, hypnotism has come a long way. What its history teaches you is that this practice has been around since prehistoric times, and it continues to be examined by incredible minds to understand how we can best use it for its full advantage.

Prehistoric Roots

Consider for a moment the ancient Indian yogic practices, such as mediation, that have become so popular today. Hypnosis and meditation are two largely separate techniques, but they have some commonalities, which you'll learn about in a later chapter. Ancient yogic practitioners used meditation as a means to achieve various results. Some practitioners used the techniques to achieve what they called enlightenment, which was the closest state of mind one could reach if one wanted to understand the tip of why we exist and what comes next. People have always tried to understand the meaning of life and the universe. Some ancient practitioners were capable of easing their minds or imaginations into a state so serene that they'd exit the immediate environment, being able to feel, see, and smell things that weren't really there. Some meditators could reach this state alone, and others were guided by a seasoned practitioner or teacher.

In a way, you can say this is a suggestion, especially if the changes to the imagined environment were guided by trained yogis. Hypnotism can be traced to numerous philosophical and religious eras in history in some form or another. Ancient Orient societies were booming with practices similar to what we know as hypnotism today. Christian mysticism was the mystical theories and practices introduced by Christians, one of which was that humans could adopt a new relationship with God, who would then bestow divinity upon them. In this sense, the theorist will change their reality and what their capabilities are by accepting a new persona. If you think about it, this practice or belief is also a suggestion. Christian mysticism isn't a religion; it's a way of thinking. You think you're changing inside and outside, therefore you are changing. When your way of thinking changes because you're following the suggestions of Christians or the Bible, you're suggestible.

Nothing negative is intended by exploring how we change our thought patterns with suggestions from books, leaders, and divine entities, but in a sense, it's a way of receiving and accepting suggestions. The same concept happened in Ancient India and China. We change who we are because of what we absorb in our environment, which in this case is what we learn from our mystic beliefs and other people. Prayer and meditation are moments we spend in silence with a heightened awareness to focus on our thoughts and changes. We make them real. Once we believe what we think or consider in our minds, we start manifesting the changes we want. Anyway, the West also used some form of hypnosis in their societies. The Stoics in Ancient Greece and Rome may also have practiced some forms of early hypnosis. Stoicism is a philosophy where we focus on promoting our virtues or inner strengths to reduce negative emotions and increase positive emotions.

Stoicism can be related to hypnosis because stoics believe they must control their minds and biases. Consider why you're interested in hypnosis. Do you want to quit smoking? Do you wish to improve your self-confidence? First, you have to overcome your biases or previous ways of thinking, and then you can work toward introducing new thought patterns. Stoics also often practiced a different form of meditation where they reflected on their thoughts logically. They'd spend time with their thoughts to understand them better, and they'd reflect on how they can change the way they think to benefit their emotions or manifest their desired habit changes. Stoicism and Pythagoreanism have some commonalities in what we believe is an early hypnosis practice. Stoics used retrospection to reflect on what needs to change and how to control their thoughts.

Pythagoreans started the practice of retrospection when Pythagoras wrote his first 'contemplation' his followers had to use before going to sleep (Mongiovi, 2017). The contemplation speaks of resting your eyes if your actions were good today. Otherwise, you need to punish yourself if your thoughts and actions were wrong. Most importantly, Pythagoreans had to meditate on their good actions and thoughts so they could sleep well. This contemplation was a way for ancient philosophers to maintain control over their minds. Pythagoras believed it was essential for people to control their minds and thoughts. Retrospection was also a way for Pythagoreans to keep their souls happy, which was thought to be seated in their emotions. All of these ancient practices were some of the first links to modern hypnosis, even though the name 'hypnosis' would only be established many centuries later.

Many hypnosis-like therapeutic practices were part of ancient societies long before it became a science. Christians, yogis, and Stoics used mystic techniques to take control of their minds and increase their awareness, but the intentions at this stage were to achieve divinity or improve the health of their souls because the soul controlled their emotions. When looking at the history of hypnosis, these groups don't often come to light. It takes a little digging to see how they used techniques similar to modern hypnosis. You'll learn about which ancient cultures are more commonly known to have practiced some form of hypnosis in the next chapter.

Scientific History

It wasn't until the eighteenth century that modern forms of hypnosis were studied, starting in Europe (Robertson, 2019). One of the first names in the scientific history of hypnosis is Franz Mesmer, a German physician. You can call him famous and infamous because his methods were intriguing yet controversial. Mesmer believed that every human, animal, and even vegetable possessed a supernatural force, which could be shared and used to heal others. He called this strategy animal magnetism. This universal energy could be transmitted to the people he 'hypnotized' so that his energy could heal their ailments. He would sit across from a patient with their knees touching as he would instruct them to focus on his eyes. He'd then use his animal magnetism to move his hands from the patient's thumbs to their shoulders.

The movements and fixation of focus caused a mesmerizing effect, much like a trance. Working with patients in Vienna and Paris, Mesmer channeled his force into the patient's body to induce an emotional crisis state. However, the scientific world wasn't interested in supernatural forces and imagined states during this time, so Mesmer's work was quickly investigated and discredited in France. Once science became the main source of evidence, and something couldn't be explained physically, matters of imagination and magnetism weren't taken seriously. Mesmer created the first type of known hypnotism called mesmerizing, and he was discredited for his wild experimentations and interests, but his work became part of later research again.

It might've been a controversial subject at the time, but mesmerism is officially the first type of scientific hypnosis. Part of what caused the controversy was also that not every patient was mesmerized, which would only be understood at a much later stage. The French were interested enough to examine different experiments with 'hypnotic' states nonetheless. Frenchman Marquis de Puységur began testing a theory of induced artificial somnambulism, which is a state of being awake and asleep at the same time. Sleepwalkers are also called somnambulists. Puységur intended to help his patients by inducing a sleep-like state that calms them to create an improved emotional state, which is kind of the opposite of an emotional crisis state. However, they'd still be fully aware and alert.

Puységur isn't a well-known name in hypnosis history, but he's one of the earlier scientific hypnosis founders. Just like Mesmer's ideas seemed supernatural and unexplainable, Puységur's ideas had the same effect. English professor John Elliotson attempted to research animal magnetism again toward the late eighteenth century, but his demonstration didn't go well, which led to the *Lancet Journal* calling him a charlatan. Elliotson may have fallen short in the demonstration, which would still only be understood much later, but he was the leading contender against the man who officially became the pioneer for hypnotism. James Braid opposed ideas of animal magnetism and Mesmer's work. He was a man of science alone, but that didn't mean he wasn't intrigued by the idea of hypnotizing people. In fact, Braid was the person who officially named the practice 'hypnotism' and 'hypnosis,' which was derived from the ancient Greek God of sleep, Hypnos (Hammer, 2019).

Braid began modifying older techniques like mesmerism to work without animal magnetism during the early to mid-nineteenth century. Braid realized he could also use the concept of focused attention to get his patients into an induced state, which would then be followed by verbal suggestions to deepen their state of mind. This is one of the closest forms of historical hypnosis techniques compared to what we use today. Using his voice and keeping his patients actively focused on something, Braid successfully managed to induce a trance-like state. What gave credence to Braid's technique was that his patients could be physically induced in minutes by simply fixating their attention on common household items. It was a natural occurrence for these people to fall into a trance-like state, and Braid was able to demonstrate this successfully. He was also able to use science to explain what happened.

The science or modern world relies on facts, but discrediting earlier theories can't be conclusive. Sometimes, we just need a fresh outlook on old theories. Hippolyte Bernheim and Ambroise-Auguste Liébeault took a step back to Mesmer's theory and combined it in an early version of a new hypnosis used at the Nancy School of Hypnotism. Liébeault was interested in combining the power of suggestions from Braid's theory with a newer model of mesmerism. Bernheim applied credibility to both theories by examining the psychological factors of what made hypnosis work. Psychology was a large interest in science during the early nineteenth century, so it gave researchers a way to understand how mesmerism in the case of fixation and suggestions worked.

The newer version of mesmerism included Braid's work of suggestions and suggestibility. Bernheim and Liébeault believed that no physical forces or physiological processes influenced a hypnotic state. Their argument was based solely on how the mind conditions perceptions through suggestions, which mediate a psychological response in the human mind. Ivan Pavlov was a Nobel-Prize winning physiologist who also made his mark on hypnosis in the mid-nineteenth century. Pavlov was famous for studying conditioned reflexes in animals, such as getting a dog to salivate when they hear a bell ring. First, the dog's mind has to be conditioned to expect food after hearing a bell. Then, the dog will produce saliva, even if there's no food in sight. Pavlov realized that similar constructs could be at play in hypnosis. Pavlov's work with hypnosis became the common Soviet method used for decades.

Finally, the scientific timeline for hypnosis was focusing on psychological changes when the mind is triggered by cues. These cues were most noticeably verbal suggestions at this time, but that would also change at a later stage. Verbal suggestions are just a small part of what triggers a response in our minds. One could almost say that an object in our environment can also be used as a suggestion, making it understandable when we focus our attention on an item to become trance-like. The human mind is always looking to perceive what our eyes see or our ears hear. It needs to process information to make us perceive how we feel and think. However, at this stage in history, suggestions were known to be verbal.

Thriving Momentum

Hypnosis was no longer a construct of sorcery or hogwash. It was becoming an interesting topic scientists and psychologists wished to understand better. Hypnosis was becoming a widely popular topic of investigation in Europe at this point, and that's how another famous name entered the timeline. Neurologist Sigmund Freud is commonly known for the iceberg theory, but he also dabbled in hypnosis after visiting Europe (Young, 2019). Freud was a psychoanalyst deeply interested in the different parts of the mind, now known as the subconscious, preconscious, and conscious minds. This is how the iceberg theory was developed because he learned that what we're consciously aware of in our minds at any time is merely the tip of an iceberg. Everything beneath that exists but isn't easily accessible.

Freud was impressed when he saw the therapeutic potential of hypnosis, and he began experimenting with it. Freud tried to resurrect different states of consciousness to reveal information from the subconscious mind with hypnosis. Reaching the subconscious mind could help patients produce varying fantasies and find information that was previously hidden from the conscious mind. Freud's experiments were largely based on the Breuer hypnosis method designed by Josef Breuer in the late nineteenth century. Breuer's theory was that patients expressed their mental well-being based on repressed traumas stuck in their subconscious minds. They aren't always aware of the traumas, but that doesn't mean they aren't affected by them. Freud used Breuer's method, but he didn't believe patients would be induced into a sleep state like Breuer.

Freud used Breuer's method to open a doorway to a lower consciousness without inducing sleep so that his patients could relive memories nonetheless. He was mainly interested in free association, which relates better to Breuer's concept of fantasies and not a trance state. Dreams or revealed memories are associated with emotions within the subconscious mind, and surfacing them can help patients recover from traumatic experiences that impact their well-being. Free association means that the consciousnesses can express themselves freely without censorship. The subconscious mind may associate various images when hearing a word. For example, if you say 'gun,' the subconscious mind may cause panic in your emotions because of past trauma. You might also immediately think about the sound of a gunshot.

Free associations reveal negative or traumatic responses in the subconscious mind. Freud and Breuer co-authored a book called *Studies on Hysteria* in 1895, which outlined the hypnotic regression therapy they used. Freud had some success with hypnosis, even helping soldiers during both World Wars, but he later dismissed his experiments and returned to his work in psychoanalysis. His doubts surrounding being able to induce some patients made him forgo his mentor's hypnosis methods and stick to psychoanalysis, of which free association is still a large part today. Not long after Freud, Emile Coué who worked at the Nancy School of Hypnotism developed a new theory called conscious autosuggestion. Coué believed that hypnosis could be self-induced, albeit he also strongly advocated against the fact that it induces a trance-like state.

Coué opened his own school of hypnosis, intending to teach people how to hypnotize themselves. His self-help method, called autosuggestion, is when someone makes suggestions to guide their own thoughts, feelings, and imagined experiences to produce hypnotic results. Coué toured America and Europe to spread the word of how people could help themselves with this newly popular technique in the early twentieth century.

Another name known in hypnosis history is Pierre Janet, also known as the father of psychotherapy. Even though Freud created the iceberg theory, Janet officially named the subconscious mind. Freud called it the unconscious mind, which stirred some confusion as being unconscious means that you're not aware of your surroundings. Ironically, Freud called the subconscious mind an unconscious plain, but he never believed in sleep-like states in hypnosis. The confusion is understandable.

Anyway, Janet also developed a theory about psychological dissociation where we disconnect ourselves from our thoughts, emotions, and experiences. In a sense, it's similar to free association because dissociation treatment is used similarly to regression therapy today. Both types of hypnosis have similar intentions, which were to reveal repressed information in the subconscious mind. People with amnesia and dissociative personality disorder have repressed memories or information in the subconscious mind, so Janet's famous dissociation therapy can help bring clarity to dissociated consciousnesses. The point is that Janet may be famous for psychotherapy, but his work was largely influenced by hypnosis. Clark Hull was a behavioral psychologist and president of the American Psychological Association (APA) in the early twentieth century. He's known as the first man to publish research related to hypnosis in a scientific journal.

Milton Erickson also stepped into the light. He's known for the popular Ericksonian hypnosis technique, which uses indirect suggestions. Erickson's method allowed for vague or guiding suggestions rather than fixed suggestions. For example, he'd give a patient permission to induce hypnosis, but it was the patient's decision whether it happened or not. In a sense, Erickson's method was guided by a hypnotherapist, but the patients maintained full control. This allowed patients to not fear hypnosis like people did in the past. One can't easily fear something if you're in control of it. Ernest Hilgard was another essential name in hypnosis history because he developed a theory and matching measurement scales that could help people understand why they can't be hypnotized as easily as someone else.

Hilgard was a professor at Stanford University, and he realized that some people appear more suggestible than others, so he developed scales that could measure susceptibility with his colleague André Weitzenhoffer. Theodore Sarbin also developed a scale of measurement, and he unraveled the ability of people to role-play in nonstate hypnosis, which is when a trance-like state isn't induced. It's rather a state of increased conscious awareness. Sabin's role-play theory was socially and psychologically useful, and it's widely used in cognitive-behavioral hypnosis today. Martin Orne researched nonstate hypnosis to ensure that false memories aren't unraveled with free association because this could cause problems in police investigations. Free association may also cause connections of no logical source. That's why psychotherapists use nonstate hypnosis instead of trance-like hypnosis.

Theodore Barber further expanded on nonstate hypnosis and is famously known for developing the modern form of cognitive-behavioral hypnosis. Barber's research proved that suggestions can also trigger psychological responses without inducing a trance-like state of mind. Indeed, some people respond better to the traditional sense of hypnosis, but others can be suggestible to nonstate hypnosis. Psychological processes like cognitive and behavioral changes can happen without the trance-like state. Imagination, motivation, and expectations can be changed without inducing traditional hypnosis. Nicholas Spanos continued the investigation into nonstate hypnosis in the latter half of the twentieth century. He introduced methods like role-modeling and learning through trial and error to the cognitive-behavioral hypnosis techniques. Even regular cognitive-behavioral therapy (CBT) uses these techniques to help patients unravel their thoughts.

From autosuggestions to nonstate hypnosis, and from indirect suggestions to changing our beliefs with affirmations, it all comes down to research conducted on the human mind and the psychology of hypnosis. Hypnosis has become popular in many fields of research now, making it more credible. Hypnosis is a cognitive skill, even used widely in many psychology fields. For all you know, your therapist might be making suggestions without even inducing a traditional hypnotic trance. The way hypnosis works on a cognitive level will be better explained in Chapter 5. However, you know how widely it's used now. It may even be used by a regular person you meet for dinner without you knowing it. The many modern methods of hypnosis will be discussed later. As you can see, many names we think are popular for other reliable fields of science have also been involved in hypnosis research. Whether they were discredited or not, their work influenced what we practice today.

Chapter 2:

How Hypnosis Has Evolved Over Time

The history of hypnosis mentions names, theories, and vague techniques because it relies mainly on scientific data. However, when you learn about the practical evolution of how hypnosis progressed from ancient traditions to stages that had spectators in awe, you finally see how hypnotism can be used for numerous results. From healing ill-health and complementing modern medicine to achieving greater goals, hypnosis has been a reliable source of results. Now, you get to learn about the details of how it was used in some form during ancient times and how this has evolved as people became more curious about the possibilities of hypnosis.

Surprising Practices

Today's research shows that interesting traditions and rituals found to have similarities with hypnosis were used by various cultures since about 5,000 years ago (Reeves, n.d.). The intentions set forth by ancient cultures practicing these intriguing rituals are known to be the earliest forms of hypnosis. One of the earliest traditions started in the temple of priest Imhotep in Ancient Egypt, which was situated in the city of Saqqara. Imhotep was also an architect and the first known physician. He served Pharaoh Zoser who ruled between 2560 and 2590 BC. Imhotep is also the Egyptian who built the first pyramid, known as the "Step Pyramid." Being the only physician at first, he was overwhelmed with patients seeking help for physical and mental ailments. Psychology wasn't well understood at this time, but it was understood that feelings of sadness and anger were mental ailments.

Imhotep would use incantations, movements, and herbal remedies to induce patients into a dream state in sleep or dream temples. The incantations are suggestions in this case. Imhotep would also use suggestions just before the patient falls asleep in a darkened part of the temple where they can dream freely. This was done in the hopes of the Egyptian gods providing a cure in the patient's dreams. Imhotep would then interpret the dreams when patients woke up and advise them on how to correct their ailment. Imhotep became a well-respected healer, and the ritual spread to other places, including Africa and Greece. Africans started practicing a similar concept called shrine sleep. Greeks began building sleep temples, which were specifically dedicated to their god of healing, Aesculapius. The Greeks used snakes in the sleep chambers as this symbolized their gods.

Asclepios was a famous Greek healer, who also later became a demi-god. More temples were erected after his death because he brought healing to the people. Priests would use incantations to help induce a trance-like state for people entering temples so they could receive the miraculous cures from Asclepios in their dreams. The priests called this early form of induction 'incubation,' derived from Latin, meaning to be on top and to lie down. Some Greeks would remain in this state for three days while the priests attempted to help them find the cure presented by Asclepios. To the Greeks, temples were a place of healing, divinity, and mysterious powers. The people showing up to the temples weren't called patients. They were called seekers. Marble walls led into the temples, on which inscriptions of previous healing journeys were recorded.

Some inscriptions spoke of lame people being able to walk again after experiencing the magical dream ritual. Seekers also had a process before they could enter the temple. They would bathe, meditate, and perform a cleansing of mind, body, and soul first. A seeker would then take their sacred skin from outside to lie down in the main temple and regenerate themselves, physically, mentally, and emotionally. A priest would help them interpret the dreams when they woke up because often the dreams were symbolic. As the ritual evolved, seekers believed that they awoke their true selves in this sleep state. Much of what happened in temples in Egypt and Greece is known as suggestion therapy, or hypnosis today.

Using sensory overload and direct suggestions, these ancient peoples were induced into a trance-like state, and many of them returned from it feeling like new people. The ancient records show that physical and emotional healing took place under the careful guidance of priests and healers. Oracles also partook in these rituals by visiting the temples. An oracle was a middle man who worked through vessels, or seekers, to receive answers from the gods. These answers would be taken to famous emperors and pharaohs. In many cases, the oracles also underwent the tradition to seek hints of the future from the gods. Oracles also experienced sensory overload, herbal mixtures, and suggestions, some of them could autosuggest themselves into the dream state while others were guided by priests in the temples. Sibyls were also placed in temples to connect with the god Apollo. These women often advised leaders during this period.

Even Alexander the Great sought advice from an oracle in Egypt before he went on his pursuit of conquering Persia. The oracle could've changed history if the message was any different from what Alexander the Great received. The deep state in which these ancient practitioners managed to connect to their gods is called Kavanah, which requires relaxation, focused attention, and motivation. All seekers, sick people, and oracles had to arrive with the right motivation, or the ritual wouldn't work. These traditions spread into Britain, too. A sleep temple was excavated in Gloucestershire, which has become a tourist attraction. Other than the sleep traditions used for healing and guidance among these ancient cultures, some simpler entertainment rituals can also be considered early forms of hypnosis.

Think about a fire-walker. They change their state of consciousness to do what they do. This entertainment ritual is also ancient. These trance-inducing traditions spread throughout Europe and all cultures. Many cultures used methods similar to modern-day hypnosis, but the sleep chambers and dream states that originated 5,000 years ago are the beginnings of what we use today.

Periodic Applications

Around the time mesmerism was being investigated upon orders from King Louis XVI, Franz Mesmer's work was still proving to be effective, even if his method would temporarily fall (Hypnosis Motivation Institute, n.d.-c). The king's orders were that a medical panel from Paris and an assortment of strange scientists discredit Mesmer's work once and for all. What people didn't realize at this time was that Mesmer's animal magnetism concept was based on Isaac Newton's laws of universal gravitation and motion. The panel of medical experts included Doctor Joseph Guillotin who invented the infamous guillotine and Antoine Lavoisier who discovered oxygen and hydrogen. It was this panel that decided Mesmer's universal fluid didn't physically exist. This is what shed doubt over Mesmer's work, but not only did he manage to mesmerize people successfully, he also influenced other great names to further investigate his methods.

This is where French Aristocrat Marquis de Puységur came into play in the 1780s. Puységur was determined to prove that Mesmer's work wasn't hogwash. He's famous for a mesmerizing session he conducted on a peasant called Victor. The young man had severe pain in his chest. Puységur was most intrigued by Victor falling into what appeared to be a sleep state after a few moments of mesmerizing him. Victor seemed to be peaceful and without convulsions from the pain in his chest, but he was still able to talk and respond to Puységur. Victor even began talking about his private affairs, which was later realized that he might've been experiencing an anxiety attack. Victor became sad in this state, but Puységur consoled him by sharing happy thoughts and a lively humming tune. Victor started singing with Puységur, who then left Victor to properly sleep for an hour. Upon waking, Victor's symptoms were gone. This is the first evidence that mesmerism successfully helped someone decrease psychological and physical symptoms.

It was after this experience with the peasant that Puységur started studying artificial somnambulism. To Puységur, the peasant showed many commonalities to someone who sleepwalks. By 1819, Abbe Faria published his life's work surrounding mesmerism, somnambulism, and what he coined "lucid dreams." Faria's journey was interesting. He fled to France to escape the revolution in India, but he was thrown in prison for 20 years by Napoleon Bonaparte. After serving his term, he became deeply fascinated with mesmerism, even though it was highly controversial. A priest and doctor of theology, Faria's book was called *On the Cause of Lucid Sleep*, and it explained how this state was reached through visual fixation that causes mental fatigue. As mesmerism and the clinical research of hypnosis progressed, a few more strange but positive applications occurred.

According to research published in the *American Journal of Clinical Hypnosis*, the first major application of mesmerism techniques was used on April 12, 1829, by surgeon Jules Cloquet in Paris (Gravitz, 1988). A female patient with breast cancer was to undergo surgery by Cloquet, and he worked with a mesmerist only known as Chapelain to forgo the use of anesthesia during the procedure. Chapelain induced the patient into a trance-like state for days before the surgery to ensure that she would successfully go under. The patient successfully reached the artificial somnambulism state where she was able to still talk about the surgery, albeit it was mumbled. She felt no fear while induced into a mesmeric state, and she showed no signs of discomfort during the procedure. Her breathing, pulse, and tone of voice also remained consistent.

Cloquet couldn't believe the controversy around mesmerism after he completed the surgery without problems. He was not the only medical professional to successfully use hypnosis instead of anesthesia. A dentist in Boston used hypnosis during dental surgery in 1836, and hypnoanesthesia became a common practice in England two years later. It was just after this in 1841 that James Braid took an interest in hypnosis. Braid spent years studying mesmerized individuals, and he concluded that it wasn't animal magnetism that caused the hypnotic state. It was changes in the neural network that induced someone into a trance. In the 1880s, Sigmund Freud changed his field from neurology to psychology after dabbling in hypnosis research. This is the time when Freud, Josef Breuer, and Emile Coué turned hypnosis into a credible practice as you learned in the last chapter.

Another subject of interest and research during the credible evolution was shamanism. Research surrounding shaman rituals was published in the *Online Journal of Complementary & Alternative Medicine* (Krippner et al., 2019). Much of the rituals practiced by shamans were hypnotic, making it easy to understand why researchers during the late nineteenth century focused on these cultures. A shaman is a healer who uses spirit forces to manipulate the recovery process for patients, and they can also experience visions of what the future holds. Indeed, this doesn't sound scientific, but the journal explains how many of their rituals influenced the evolution of hypnotism. Shamans used rhythmic chanting, dancing, colorful costumes, and the beating of drums to induce patients into a trance-like state. They often used sensory overload to induce hypnosis, similar to the ancient Greeks.

Shamanism is practiced in Africa, Asia, and some South American countries, but a similar concept was used by Native Americans for a long time. Native Americans used the Ghost Dance to create a trance-inducing movement. In a sense, this induction dance, song, and drum beats acted as a coping mechanism for Native Americans when settlers arrived.

Whether hypnotism was used as a healing ritual or physicians used it to replace anesthesia, there's no doubt that many practices we think are strange have certainly influenced the research growing in hypnosis. The history of hypnosis is one thing, but knowing how the modern forms of hypnosis were influenced by cultural traditions and curious minds is another thing altogether. Humans have always been curious about changing their minds, the way they feel, and what their decisions should be in the future.

From oracles to shamans, hypnosis in some form was used to determine the best move forward. From sleep temples to Victor the peasant, hypnosis also proves to have healing benefits. How much healing can be achieved with hypnosis is still to come.

Modern Expansion

When something works, it draws people's attention. As the concept of hypnosis gained more popularity in the twentieth century, expanding into areas like psychology and self-help, the research pivoted, and the practice became more interesting. Around the 1920s, hypnosis was expanding into various fields, even entertainment (Hypnosis Motivation Institute, n.d.-b). Vaudeville acts were popular during this time, and among the actors, comedians, musicians, and ventriloquists, stage hypnotism entered the lives of regular people. From hypnotists getting people to do what they asked to mentalists encouraging someone from the audience to miraculously choose a pre-established number, hypnosis was finally entering the lives of people outside the science world. Some entertainers had people barking like dogs, and others had them doing the most embarrassing things on stage.

Dave Elman was one such stage mesmerist who had people in stitches. He later became a hypnotherapist who wrote the manual called *Hypnotherapy*. Elman was a great performer, but his manual is still one of the most reliable sources of learning about hypnosis today. Many stage performers had their audience believing that hypnosis was trickery or magic. It was new to people, and anything new is suspicious. It was around this time when Clark Hull was conducting a large-scale study of the phenomena at the University of Wisconsin. Hull published *Hypnosis and Suggestibility* in 1933, which also became a reliable source of evidence as it was backed by numerous studies and clinical trials. It was Hull who officially confirmed that hypnosis was an entirely different state of mind to sleep, even though they seemed similar. Moreover, hypnosis didn't give the induced person any superpowers or extraordinary abilities. They could still only do what was within their reasonable and realistic capacity.

In this sense, even a stage performer couldn't hypnotize someone to do the splits unless they were flexible enough. Hypnosis is a realistic concept. It's not some magical construct that allows us to be superhumans. It can help us gradually progress toward what we want, but it can't make us skinny overnight just because a hypnotist told us we'll lose 50 pounds. That's not how hypnosis works, and once you understand how rational the process is, you'll know what you can achieve. However, Hull clarified this part of the newly trending entertainment tradition. He provided evidence to show that hypnosis is not magic or trickery. It's a skill, either applied by someone to themselves with autosuggestions, or it's applied by someone who can hypnotize someone else. The human brain can heal physical and mental challenges, and hypnosis is about controlling the brain. It's not hypnosis that heals people. It's their control over their brains that do the job.

Take Milton Erickson as one example of a hypnosis enthusiast who used the practice to manage something his brain was capable of doing. Erickson was a student of Hull, and he became fascinated by the potentials for hypnosis due to his muscular stiffness and pain caused by polio when he was a child. Erickson began teaching himself to induce and control his mind to reduce the pain he suffered. His techniques were similar to autosuggestion. As Erickson trained his mind to manage the pain and stiffness, his life became a lot more pleasant. His fascination turned into work as he's known as one of the twentieth century hypnosis pioneers. For some hypnotherapists, personal experience with the practice showed them how effective it could be, so they became determined to research the possibilities of hypnosis beyond their crutches. America also became more familiar with hypnosis by the Second World War.

Any ideas of magic and trickery were nearly gone as schools for hypnosis were popping up during the mid-twentieth century. Hypnosis remains a popular stage performance, but people are understanding it better now. Hypnosis was even used to successfully treat trauma, dissociation, phobias, and anxiety during the Second World War. American institutions were using a technique called abreaction, which requires a hypnotist to return soldiers to their traumas so they could relive them in the hopes of venting out the psychological issues. Abreaction isn't the most popular method used today, but it proved successful among countless injured soldiers. Hypnosis was finally becoming an accepted practice across the world, including America. Even the media stopped connecting hypnosis to frightening Svengali imagery when the twenty-first century came around.

Hypnosis is seen as a means to achieve better mental health, and many practitioners manage to pursue goals they once struggled with because they have control over their minds. Motivation and persistence are hard to come by when you have no control over your mind. They can come and go, which doesn't take you any closer to what you truly desire. All the names associated with the evolution of hypnosis could never have imagined the potentials it would bring. Mesmer never thought people would quit smoking or drinking, and Braid never imagined that hypnosis could help people gain confidence. Cloquet must have been afraid of attempting surgery on a woman who wasn't under anesthesia, but he did it anyway, and he proved that it could be done. Many surgeons followed him. The secret that might not have been too clear at this stage was that the human brain controls everything from pain management to habit formation.

Hypnosis has the potential to connect our consciousnesses and produce our desired effects. There's nothing wrong with the stage performers in Las Vegas. Entertainment is what keeps us alive, but hypnosis is so much more than this. Once you realize that hypnosis is not just an act or an outdated ritual performed by ancient cultures, you'll finally see the potential it has for your growth. Moreover, hypnosis can be self-applied once you learn about the simple ways to induce and anchor yourself. Suggestions are also just a part of the process, and they're entirely controlled by what you desire. Hypnosis is in some sense a way for you to communicate directly with all the consciousnesses in your brain so you can achieve what matters deeply to you, and best of all is that you have scientifically proven ways to master your mind as you deem necessary.

Chapter 3:

Defining Hypnosis

The average Joe doesn't greatly comprehend what hypnosis really is, and many myths and false truths surround the practice. The ongoing presence of stage performers makes it more challenging to recognize hypnosis for what it is. Movies don't make the practice easy to understand, either, but one must always remember that movies are fiction. *The Manchurian Candidate*, *Old Boy*, and *Dead Again* are poor examples of what hypnosis looks like. Humanity has a problem if we start believing what we see in movies. Nonetheless, understand what hypnosis is and isn't, and your journey to learning how to hypnotize yourself will be concise and fruitful.

The Face of Hypnosis

When deciding whether hypnosis is for you and how you can practice it, the best start of any new journey is with knowledge. Hypnosis for entertainment purposes must be just that. Never consider stage performances and movies to build your knowledge for a subject clearly outlined by science and psychology. There are too many stereotypical untruths making the rounds, so you must understand what hypnosis is. According to the American Psychological Association (APA, 2021), hypnosis is a therapeutic technique in which clinicians make suggestions to individuals who have undergone a procedure designed to relax them and focus their minds. The majority of clinicians agree that hypnosis is a powerful and effective tool in therapy, despite the controversies around it. It has successfully been used to manage pain, reduce anxiety, heal gastrointestinal disorders, and fight depression to name a few benefits. This is what hypnosis looks like in clinical terms.

In clinical and personal use, hypnosis acts as a cognitive skill that helps you modulate certain psychological and neurological factors. The factors you learn to control include learning to engage with your imagination, setting new expectations within reason, and motivating yourself to pursue goals. You develop an anti-volition against obstacles stopping you from behaving and thinking the way you desire. You break through inhibitions with a simple technique called 'suggestion.' It doesn't matter what type of hypnosis you experience or practice. It also doesn't matter if you're practicing self-hypnosis or visiting a hypnotherapist. Suggestions are the cornerstone of what makes it work, and believe it or not, the suggestions belong to you. You'll never do things you don't want to. However, once your mind is relaxed, and those inhibitions are reduced, you'll be more likely to listen and respond to suggestions.

The biggest challenge preventing people from learning self-hypnosis is that misinformation creates new inhibitions. People question whether hypnosis is genuine. They wonder whether they can benefit, or is this practice merely a trick for gullible individuals? They brush the practice off. The truth is that the cognitive skills developed in hypnosis open new doorways for you. Expecting anything but what happens in real life hypnosis will only set you up for disappointment. Your inhibitions will grow and block you from developing the hypnosis skill. Making a conscious decision to give it a shot, expecting the true nature of what you're about to experience, and being open to becoming suggestible are three ways you can ensure that hypnosis works in a clinical or personal sense. You're in charge of how it changes your life, well-being, and habits. Let's debunk the most common myths that have people doubting hypnosis.

Myth 1: Hypnosis Induces a Different State of Mind or Consciousness

Understandably, people get confused when they watch hypnosis in action. They think people are induced into a deep sleep state where their awareness and inhibitions are removed. Hypnosis is not a change in the state of your mind, even though some people reach a trance-like state. It's not a state in the sense of a different consciousness taking over while your conscious mind rests. Hypnosis can contract and expand your awareness, but generally, you're fully conscious of what's happening while you're in this trance-like relaxation. Sigmund Freud's work with the three consciousnesses and his dabbling in hypnosis can also cause confusion, but Freud never confirmed any such theory as a change in state of mind. Freud knew about the subconscious mind, which is currently below our awareness on regular days.

Freud experimented with how hypnosis opens the subconscious mind to our awareness, but the conscious mind doesn't sleep. That's a misconception. All your minds are wide awake during hypnosis. Hypnotherapy patients do not reach a state of stupor where they follow silly orders because they lack control. They're in complete control during the entire procedure. Their focus also doesn't particularly turn into the subconscious mind; they just become more aware of what's hidden inside of it while they maintain their full cognitive abilities in the conscious mind. One great challenge in psychology is that people don't know how to allow the conscious and subconscious minds to communicate effectively. Hypnosis can close this gap, allowing you to make suggestions directly to the subconscious mind while your conscious mind stands by for reasoning.

Our conscious minds are inactive when we sleep, leaving the subconscious mind to do its thing, but hypnosis brings the two together while listening to suggestions or autosuggestions. Stage hypnosis is a good example of how this practice doesn't change our state of mind. The hypnotist will make suggestions to their 'victim,' maybe asking them to bark like a dog.

The 'victim' is entirely aware of the ridiculous suggestion, and they're capable of rejecting it, but they don't reject it because their inhibitions are down. All the inhibitions that would've told them not to bark like a dog in front of an audience are gone. They feel more comfortable and relaxed to carry out the suggestion for entertainment and never lose their free will. Hypnotists can't control your mind; only you can do that.

Without the fears and inhibitions preventing you from partaking in the fun, chances are you'll probably bark. That's why relaxation is part of the practice. Relaxing your mind and body allows you to drop your inhibitions, but you can always step back if you're about to do something you don't want to. When you understand that hypnosis doesn't change your mental state, you realize that making suggestions is merely a form of highly effective communication with all parts of your mind, which are now fully aware and alert. Whether you make the suggestions or a hypnotherapist helps you, you're simply communicating directly with your brain that's listening intently and not worrying about simple inhibitions.

Myth 2: Hypnosis and Meditation Must Be One of the Same

This is entirely incorrect. The two practices have some commonalities. For example, both techniques can use suggestion and relaxation to bring calmness or guidance to someone learning to practice them, but the goal of each technique is different. Meditation is based mainly on mindfulness, which is the observation and acceptance of random thoughts and feelings. People aren't recommended to judge their thoughts or even change them. Mindfulness is also about being present and experiencing everything in real-time through your senses. Using suggestions with meditation can be useful in guided sessions where someone sits on a beach and experiences the scene with their senses, but you can't use suggestions to change your thoughts in mindful meditation because then you're not accepting them or yourself.

On the other hand, hypnosis relies mainly on suggestions. You can indeed induce a state of calmness and relaxation that helps you become more suggestible, but your sessions have a purpose. You want to suggest changes to your thoughts, habits, and beliefs. You're constantly interacting with the associations between the conscious and subconscious minds by making suggestions. Hypnosis isn't about sitting in silence. It's about expressing ideas and suggestions while your awareness of all the minds is expanded. You don't intend to change your state of mind, which is often a meditative habit among seasoned practitioners. Indeed, varying states of mind can be more conducive to learning new skills and beliefs, but you don't have to enter a trance state to communicate effectively with your brain. Relaxing before making suggestions opens your mind and lowers your inhibitions. As a seasoned self-hypnosis practitioner, you can practice deepening techniques to induce a somnambulist state if you desire it.

Myth 3: Too Few People Are Genuinely Suggestible

Ask yourself, are you confident in your work, and do you exceed in your work? If the answer to both questions is yes, then you kind of debunked the myth yourself. Humans have incredible abilities when they believe in themselves and the way they do things. You exceed yourself at work because you're willing to apply the methods that you're comfortable with. Hypnosis is not so comfortable if you're new to the practice. According to Doctor Lynn Ponton (2016), only five to ten percent of people are highly suggestible, but that doesn't mean hypnosis isn't for you, even if you fall into the doubtful group. Being highly suggestible refers to people who can undergo surgical procedures after hypnosis, much like the woman with breast cancer. Being able to forgo anesthesia and opt for hypnosis requires one crucial factor. The patient must be willing and confident that hypnosis works.

What you believe is what makes you more suggestible to hypnosis. Even though so few people are highly suggestible, between 60 and 79 percent of people are moderately suggestible, which means they can be induced by a stage performer or hypnotherapist. Suddenly, the numbers don't look so low anymore. It's only around 25 to 30 percent of people who are minimally suggestible, but that can change. The greater your belief grows, the more suggestible you become. There are also varying stages of hypnosis, and you might only be induced to the lesser stage if your hypnosis confidence still has to grow. However, the more you practice it, and the better your experiences become, the more open you become to the higher suggestibility bracket. Remember that hypnosis is a process of lowering your inhibitions. Not having confidence in the practice automatically erects inhibitions preventing you from experiencing it to your greatest benefit.

Hypnosis can only work wonders for someone who becomes confident in the process. You might never be able to replace anesthesia with hypnosis, but you can reach the moderate suggestibility most people experience after practicing it. Go back to your work for a moment. Would you have answered yes to both questions on your first day? No, you wouldn't have had any confidence in your process or abilities. Give it time, and allow your unique process to build confidence. Hypnotherapists know that every person is unique as well. They understand how different people respond to varying language suggestions. Different people don't associate with the same suggestions. This happens because our brains process unique associations and language cues.

You and I won't think of the same thing when we hear the same word. Our memories and experiences differ. Our brains speak different languages. Good hypnotherapists understand this, so they spend time learning your language first. They might ask you questions that allow them to distinguish keyword patterns in your language. They don't use predetermined scripts anyone can find on Google. They cater to the uniqueness of each patient. If you've tried self-hypnosis before, and it failed, you might also want to query whether you used generic online scripts. In truth, between building confidence and catering to your unique mental language associations, you'll be as suggestible as you desire. Everyone is suggestible if they practice self-hypnosis right or they visit a non-generic hypnotherapist. Trust is another factor you must consider if you're using a hypnotherapist. You won't be suggestible to someone you don't trust.

That's why so many people are turning to self-hypnosis. It allows them to maintain a full sense of control over the outcome, and they don't feel like someone will manipulate them in a way that makes them uncomfortable. American hypnotherapists are strictly guided by ethical laws, and they won't be suggesting that you do anything that makes you uncomfortable, but feelings of deep discomfort with your hypnotherapist could prevent you from being suggestible. Hypnotherapists aren't even allowed to touch your shoulder to induce you without asking your permission first. It's much safer than you think, but if you want to learn how to induce yourself with guidance from someone who does it daily, you can visit a hypnotherapist to build your confidence first. Finally, knowing exactly why you want to induce yourself can also make suggestibility more possible. After all, you want your communication with your mind to be concise when you expand your awareness.

Myth 4: It's All a Bunch of Pretentious Play

When you tell yourself in the morning that this day will be filled with joy, and you go through the day with a smile on your face, are you pretending to be happy? When you say to yourself that you love a good steak, and you eat it with vigor to satiate your watering mouth, are you pretending to enjoy the steak? Stage hypnosis can be seen as a form of pretending because you're having fun while acting out the suggestions of a hypnotist. However, keep in mind that you're choosing to act it out because your inhibitions are down, and you're having a ball. In this sense, hypnotism can turn us into good actors when we feel more comfortable doing what we wouldn't normally do, but it's silly to think that all hypnosis is pretentious play. If you choose to bark like a dog because someone suggests it, then you're pretending. Your acting is in no way making you do something you can't normally do if you overcame some fears first.

However, if you're using a suggestion to recall a time you felt happy, you can't possibly think this is pretending. You're merely reminding yourself that you can feel happy. You're associating your woken minds to a time you felt happy. There was no pretending the day you laughed loud enough to draw attention from the car next to you. Just as you make suggestions about past experiences that confirm what your inhibitions want to prevent you from doing, you can also use them to work toward something you're about to do. Hypnotism has nothing to do with playing pretend. That's why suggestions and expectations must be realistic. Chances are that if a hypnotist tells you to jump off a building, all so-called pretending will stop because your free will never stops working.

Hypnosis requires compliance from both parties if you're being hypnotized by someone else. Sure, you can get into the moment, but they can't make you do things that go against your moral fibers, logic, and knowledge because the conscious mind remains awake. Hypnotists can encourage unusual behavior if they find the right communication to use in suggestions, but you still won't even pretend or play along if the suggestion doesn't associate good outcomes. The bottom line is that not all hypnosis experiences can be confirmed as pretentious play.

Myth 5: Hypnosis Doesn't Change Anything on a Physical or Chemical Level

Hypnosis is a process that stimulates activity in the brain, and the brain is made of billions of neurons firing 50 to 200 times a second, making changes not only possible but also inevitable (Handel, 2009). Even a thought ignites changes in the brain, and the brain is the catalyst that changes everything in your body, including the way your body works. Hypnosis can't make your body change in impossible ways. Logic always trumps unrealistic expectations. You can't hypnotize yourself to wake up with blue eyes tomorrow if you have brown eyes. This is biologically impossible. You also can't expect your legs to grow longer or your weight to drop off overnight. Your body wasn't designed to make these changes possible, albeit some of them become possible over time with lifestyle changes, which are suggested during hypnosis. You can lose weight by suggesting it if your expectations are realistic.

You'll feel more motivated to pursue a healthier lifestyle because your brain's chemicals will change as you continue associating what you want with what you have now. Your brain will give you a boost of feel-good hormones every time you suggest getting into shape to fit back into your jeans. At the speeds your brain works, you'd think it can change things instantly, but it can't. It also can't manifest changes your body isn't capable of making. Suggesting that you grow wings to fly isn't going to happen, but making suggestions that encourage motivation to pursue improved well-being and success are rational enough to cause minor changes that add up over time. Hypnosis helps your body move toward its full potential. You can't mystically exceed human biology. Hypnosis may reveal aspects of your physical and mental ability you didn't notice before, but it can't conjure new abilities that go against being human.

Other Common Myths

Debunking the top five myths around hypnosis can help you begin your journey to practicing this valuable skill. However, a few less common myths may still cause doubt. Geneticist and psychologist Arash Emamzadeh who graduated from the University of British Columbia reviewed various myths around hypnosis and the research that debunked them (Emamzadeh, 2021).

The first myth is that some people have personality traits more likely to be suggestible than others. No personality traits are strongly related to suggestibility. An open mind, willingness to use your imagination, and being able to absorb experiences fully can help you because these are directly related to hypnosis. However, a neurotic person is not less likely to be suggestible than an extrovert. There just isn't evidence to support the fact.

The second myth is that a hypnotist has to be highly skilled to induce you. On one hand, good hypnotherapists individualize their approach to each participant. On the other hand, some hypnotherapists simply need to build rapport with you first, or you won't allow them to induce you. Remember that you're in control, and no one can drop a hat to induce you, but this also means that some hypnotherapists might find it challenging to induce you because they have no rapport with you. That's why it matters to trust your hypnotherapist. Some patients feel a lot more comfortable on the second visit, and the induction goes better.

The third myth is that you have to possess the attention of a monk to induce hypnosis successfully. Focusing all your attention on the session and suggestions can help you induce yourself quickly and efficiently, but it's not necessary if you're still learning how to practice hypnosis. Focus is a fragile concept, and our brains don't like focusing intently on one point of interest. It takes time to train your mind to focus on this level. For now, aim to relax yourself because this will naturally peak your attention to what you want to focus on.

The final myth that makes the rounds is that you'll forget what happened during your session. In formal terms, this is called posthypnotic amnesia, and the chances of it happening to someone who starts practicing self-hypnosis is zero unless you carefully place suggestions and cancellations during your session. You can pre-record sessions for yourself, in which you can suggest that certain memories are repressed. The cancellation must also be placed right after the suggestion. Saying "I remember everything" as your cancellation is one example. This will cancel the suggestion you placed during self-hypnosis if you wish to surface the memories post-hypnosis. When it comes to hypnotherapists, you can request that posthypnotic amnesia is suggested. Most people won't request this, but it's an option. Hypnotherapists can't just do it without your permission.

Another scenario that falsely creates a posthypnotic amnesia situation is when you become so relaxed that you fall asleep. Remember that your state of mind doesn't change, but you can become so relaxed in deeper hypnosis that you fall asleep. This even happens with self-hypnosis, and it's more common with highly suggestible people. The bottom line is that post-hypnosis forgetfulness is only caused by two factors. You either suggest it, which must be done with a cancellation sentence for post-hypnosis, or you fall asleep. Either way, you're still 100 percent aware during your session. Suggestions and cancellations only work because you're in a comfortable, open place where your mind is more accepting of what you're suggesting.

Now that you know what hypnosis is and isn't, you're better prepared to learn the basics of self-hypnosis.

Chapter 4:

Why and How Self-Hypnosis Works

The history and debunked myths surrounding hypnosis certainly shed new light on the practice. What it all comes down to though is that the brain is the center of what's going on during hypnosis. Structural and chemical changes do take place. Self-hypnosis is the most controversial topic when it comes to the facts about whether it works or not. Being able to induce yourself into a relaxed state so you can make suggestions to benefit you is possible and explainable. Don't allow doubts to prevent you from practicing a technique that could bring so many desired changes to your life. Instead, learn how probable self-hypnosis is for anyone who commits to it.

Self-Hypnosis Explained

There isn't much difference between hypnotherapy and self-hypnosis, considering that you're always in control of your induction and wakening. Some people are highly suggestible, making it easier for them to be induced by someone else, and with some training, they can have the same benefits of self-induction without falling asleep. Think about it this way. A hypnotherapist suggests that you close your eyes, tap your fingers against your knee, or feel the sensation of falling deeper and deeper into a relaxing space. If you close your eyes and focus on falling deeper and deeper into a calmer space, you'll have the same effect. Either way, you're allowing yourself to go deeper into a relaxing place. The hypnotherapist isn't placing you in a literal elevator and making you go down many floors. This is something entirely controlled by your imagination. Therefore, all kinds of hypnosis are self-hypnosis.

The process you experience during a session is to detach yourself from the external environment while being fully awake. Your awareness grows as your minds look inward. Awakening the subconscious mind, your conscious mind can work with it, which isn't something you can easily achieve if your focus is attached to the external environment. You stop paying attention to what's happening externally. During hypnosis, you experience a calmer state of mind that allows both minds to be aware of your internal environment. This trance-like state doesn't detach your attention from the internal working of your minds. You gain better focus, and the deep relaxation and comfort help you lower your inhibitions the subconscious mind would automatically put in place while your focus remains on the external environment. Hypnosis allows you to bypass automated processing by connecting the conscious and subconscious minds.

This heightened state of awareness can also help you focus deeply on matters that trouble you. Our minds can be so overwhelmed with everything happening around us that we can't focus properly on our troubles. Our lives become so crazy that we have to practice relaxing our minds again. A hypnotherapist guides you to relaxation because they have experience with tranquil words and visualizations that could calm you down. The suggestions they use can either be direct or indirect. Direct suggestions would be "you feel yourself going deeper" or "you can see yourself taking another step down the spiral staircase." Indirect suggestions would be "you may go deeper if you wish" and "you may take another step if you want to." The difference between direct and indirect suggestions is that the latter gives patients a greater sense of control. Direct suggestions aren't intended to force you to follow them, but some people prefer using direct cues.

A hypnotherapist will then help you anchor yourself to a relaxed state when you feel like you've reached the depth you desire. The anchor is merely an associative reminder of how it feels in this state. At this point, the hypnotherapist will start making suggestions, depending on what you wish to achieve. They might take you on a journey about how life will be different if you quit smoking if that's your intention. Smoking cessation is a common reason for people to dabble in hypnosis. Once you're in a relaxed state of mind and your inhibitions are down, this is the perfect place for the hypnotherapist to plant sprouting suggestions in favor of your intentions. They might also use this calm space to suggest coping mechanisms. Otherwise, the hypnotherapist may take you on a journey to past experiences if that was your desire discussed with them. A hypnotherapist will hypnotize you, according to your needs.

When it comes to self-hypnosis, you'll be experiencing the same process. The only difference is that you'll either guide your mind in silence, or you'll record sessions uniquely designed for what you want to achieve. Self-recorded sessions are the best because you can control how you place your anchors and cancellations if you use them. You can also make sure your desired suggestions are added. Constructing a recorded session helps, especially if you're highly suggestible and fall into deep relaxation. And if you fall asleep, that's fine. You're in your own hands, so what could go wrong? Self-hypnosis can help people become successful, heal from past trauma by practicing the right kind of hypnosis, and manage chronic pain. Not everyone can afford hypnotherapy sessions, and some people just don't have the time, but self-hypnosis allows you to control the session, your time, and your budget.

Tips for Recording

Recording your sessions makes you feel more comfortable, knowing that you're making your own suggestions. The first challenge in recording your sessions is to increase your suggestion impact. Suggestions are personal choices, and they depend wholeheartedly on what you wish to achieve. Induction suggestions will be discussed in Chapter 5, but talking yourself through the recorded session, and planting suggestions where you'll be most relaxed require some finesse. Whether your suggestions are to remember a time you felt more confident, or you want to make suggestions about living a healthier life, you need to consider tonality in the recording. Our tone of voice has more influence over ourselves and other people than anything else. Consider whether a friend responds well to you saying you're sorry for forgetting your commitment while you laugh. Our body language and tone of voice bring home any words we say.

According to the Hypnosis Training Academy (2014), the words you use only influence seven percent of your session, but body language and non-verbal cues influence a massive 55 percent and tone of voice influences your session another 38 percent. This is a fact shared in many fields of psychology because our brains interpret more than only words. Our brains also process how the words sound. Hypnosis is a time of delivering effective communication straight to your conscious and subconscious minds while their awareness is focused intently on the suggestions. Using an angry voice while recording your sessions will only confuse your mind. A calm voice is the best way you can record yourself. Calmness leads to relaxation, so a calm voice suggests a relaxed state for both minds. Your tone of voice should also be exciting enough to hold your attention. Listening to a bland voice will likely make you fall asleep.

You want positive emotions expressed in your recorded voice. An interesting study was published in the *Annual Review of Neuroscience* that explains why a tone of voice can change emotions in yourself or others (Rozzolatti & Craighero, 2004). Neuroscientist Giacomo Rozzolatti and his associates at the University of Parma in Italy discovered mirror neurons when scanning the brains of people conversing with each other. The discovery opened new doors in hypnotic suggestion because the results showed that two people's brain chemistry and wave patterns became identical, proving that they can share a precise chemical experience. Chemical changes in the brain happen when your emotions change, so talking to yourself in a relaxing voice can ignite the correct expressions in your biochemistry to help you induce hypnosis more easily. Talking in a positive voice when you make confidence suggestions in your recording can also improve your response to what you want to achieve.

Once you practice self-hypnosis enough to make your sessions go smoothly, you can also use voice inflections, which are changes of emotional tonality that relate to what you're saying. At first, you may want to stick to neutrally calm tones to practice self-hypnosis, but you can add an exciting rise in your tone of voice when you make confidence suggestions in later recordings. Even though you're listening to your own voice, you'll still be influenced by the tonality, so make it count. Hypnotherapists spend time perfecting their tonality before they get it right. Beyond tonality, you should also enunciate your words clearly. Remember that you'll be in deep relaxation, so you want your minds to hear and understand the words clearly. You should also consider timing. Listen to a few online generic scripts just to grab the concept of timing. You want a rhythm that paces you through the session. You're not racing against the clock.

Finally, your suggestions will be personal and unique, but try to stick with positive words and tones. Your subconscious mind doesn't have those automatic inhibitions in place to protect it from harsh suggestions under hypnosis. You can easily decline your confidence if you use negative suggestions. A negative suggestion would be "I don't feel stupid" or "I don't look like a walrus on the beach." Positive suggestions would be "I intend to gain more knowledge" and "I see myself slowly adopting better choices to look healthier and happier." If you're using regression styles of hypnosis, you can say something along the lines of "I'm thinking of that time I walked onto the stage like I owned the place." Avoid taking yourself back to a time of confidence with negative suggestions like "Why don't I feel as confident as I was that day?"

The way you speak to yourself during hypnosis matters. Take this practice seriously so that you use it for the many benefits it can bring. At first, your hypnosis journey will be a matter of trial and error, whether you hypnotize yourself or visit a hypnotherapist. You'll even notice how effective your hypnotherapist's tone of voice is, which may increase or decrease your suggestibility. Understandably, a boring audiobook would make you fall asleep. Listening to someone who has no emotional expression will make you look for reasons to leave. Nonetheless, your trial and error journey must be expected.

The Brain Under Hypnosis

Why and how hypnosis works for anyone dedicated to practicing it are answers you can find in the brain. Researchers at Stanford have conducted intriguing studies on the brain while people were under hypnosis (Bach, 2016). The main question the researchers wished to answer was what happens in the brain while someone experiences hypnosis. The research was led by the professor of psychiatry and behavioral sciences Daniel Spiegel. They used 57 participants, of which 21 were minimally to moderately suggestible and the other 36 participants were highly suggestible. Functional magnetic resonance imaging was used to scan the brains of the participants while under hypnosis. Spiegel and the other researchers discovered three distinct changes in the brains of highly suggestible individuals during hypnosis.

The first noticeable change was recorded in the dorsal anterior cingulate, which is the part of your brain that partially serves the connection between cognitive, or higher thinking, and motor skills. This part of the brain is also often investigated in research related to motivation, emotional regulation, motor control, and reward processing. Seeing this change on the scans explains why hypnotized individuals can still think and use cognitive responses, but highly suggestible people may become physically still. This is why people assume a trance-like state has been reached. Indeed, the person is in a deep relaxation where they'll likely only respond behaviorally to the suggestions made, but their bodies will also more likely be relaxed. Their motor control will slow down, but this doesn't mean their cognitive skills are asleep.

The second change seen on the scans was to an area connecting the dorsolateral prefrontal cortex to the insula. The connection between these regions activated more during hypnosis, which wasn't prevalent during regular resting. The dorsolateral prefrontal cortex is a small part of your prefrontal lobe to the left of your forehead. It's responsible for executive functions like attention and memory. The insula is a part of the cerebral cortex, which is found deep within the large fissure that separates the temporal, parietal, and frontal lobes on the sides of your brain. The insula plays an important role in all immune functions in the body, controlling the sympathetic and parasympathetic nervous systems. It can influence whether you feel stressed or not. It can also influence how relaxed you feel.

Siegel believes that the connection between these two brain regions makes up a large part of the mind-body connection. This connection also helps the brain process and control what's happening inside the body and brain at any moment. However, the activation of this connection also proves that attention is increased during hypnosis. Focused attention during hypnosis is largely natural for highly suggestible individuals but less natural in lower suggestibility. This doesn't mean moderate or minimally suggestible people can't focus their attention. It just means it requires more effort. Again, focused attention isn't the lifeblood of hypnosis. It's something you master over time if you're not highly suggestible yet. The parasympathetic nervous system also activates to induce deep relaxation. It switches off the stress response caused by the sympathetic nervous system.

The third observation made on the scans was that the connection between the dorsolateral prefrontal cortex and the default mode network was reduced. Remember that the dorsolateral prefrontal cortex is the executive region that controls your attention and working, or short-term, memory. The default mode network includes brain regions called the posterior cingulate cortex, medial prefrontal cortex, and angular gyrus. The medial prefrontal cortex is a highly active part of your brain, but the scans showed a reduced activity during hypnosis. This region of the brain is responsible for decision-making. It relies mostly on goal-directed behaviors in response to stimuli, but it's largely influenced by patterns in the other areas of the default mode network. The posterior cingulate cortex is located in the limbic system just above the midbrain.

This region works actively when you're doing tasks on autopilot. There isn't much more known about what the function of the posterior cingulate cortex is beyond this, but it plays a role in automatic thoughts, habits, behaviors, and decisions. Less activation in this region could indicate a lowering of your inhibitions based on automatic processing stored within the default mode network. The angular gyrus is located near the sides of your head, just above your ears. The angular gyrus is part of the parietal lobe, and it has many interesting functions as part of the default mode network. It processes information related to language, spatial data, and numbers. The connection between the entire system known as the default mode network and the dorsolateral prefrontal cortex is reduced during hypnosis. The disconnection between these regions can explain why people no longer focus their awareness on external factors, including their actions.

It can also explain why people aren't bothered as much by their previous automatic thoughts and responses. Spiegel and his associates certainly proved that hypnosis changes the brain and the way it functions. Any changes within the brain can also cause chemical changes. For example, the ability to activate the parasympathetic nervous system during deep relaxation creates a chemical response. Various chemicals flow through your body, such as serotonin and norepinephrine.

These chemicals can even have analgesic effects, which may be able to replace addictive painkillers and anti-anxiety medicine that only cause other side effects. Spiegel continues to research the neurological activations of the brain during hypnosis because combining this with carefully curated brain stimulation could reduce the need for prescription drugs. It can also reduce the need for anxiety treatments and pain management strategies.

Spielberg and his associates at Stanford will continue to examine how these results can work in new therapeutic treatments. Spielberg's study was incredibly eye-opening, even though the results were more in favor of highly suggestible people. You have to remember that you can become more suggestible with practice and vigorous intention. No one can achieve anything without practice. Some people will be induced much easier than others, but practice makes perfect. On the other hand, suggestibility is also measured on scales before someone's induced. That's where research by the Department of Psychology at the University of Connecticut changed the playing field (Kirsch, 1997).

Researchers evaluated the way suggestibility is measured, and they found that people are categorized by their hypnotizability before they go under. Many measuring scales are self-reports, or they mark specific personality traits. This becomes challenging because suggestibility is not more likely to occur in one personality than another. Nonetheless, the results of the research concluded that these scales better measure waking suggestibility than hypnotic suggestibility. Once induced to any degree, most people are suggestible enough to benefit from hypnosis, and they deepen their relaxed state as they continue to practice it.

Reluctancy is a sensitive topic in hypnosis. People are reluctant because they believe it can't work for them. However, reluctance is merely a habit brought forward by inhibitions. Reluctant people don't easily intend to be hypnotized. The fortunate news is that any habit can be changed neurologically. You still might never reach the deepest stage of relaxation where your brain scans would match those of highly suggestible people, but you can come as close as your willingness allows. Habits are also born in the brain. Research published in the *Oxford Research Encyclopedia of Psychology* sheds some light on habits and behavioral changes (Gardner & Rebar, 2019). The default mode network is responsible for choosing automatic responses and decisions. The response counteracts a cue, and in most cases, it's swift and automatic.

Our behavior and thought patterns are designed from an early age. The more we practice something, the more information is stored within the basal ganglia in the midbrain. The information stored here relies on associations to resurface it, so a cue acts as an association that the default mode network uses to make a quick and effortless decision. For example, your alarm clock rings, so you wake up. The ringer is the cue. Another example is when you hear the name of your favorite food and you feel a craving for it. The word was the cue in this case. What the researchers found was that cues are important in habit changes in the brain. What follows the cues is so fast and efficient that you spend little to no energy on responding to the cue. Intentions and executive functions like attention play no role in this default response. The only time you stop the automatic response is if you *intentionally focus* on the decision you want to make. You must consciously decide that you'll respond in a certain way.

This also relates to the practice of hypnosis or self-hypnosis. You must commit to practicing it because it won't become an automatic habit if you don't put in the conscious effort. Prolonged and consistent practice, with failure or success, will slowly turn it into a habit. Once you build a habit, your default mode network will automatically allow your attention to be part of the process. It will slow down, allowing the brain to focus on the session. This only happens with time, especially if you're reluctant to use hypnosis. The only missing piece is the cue. Hypnosis and self-hypnosis use various cues. Suggestions are cues you'll grow familiar with when you become more comfortable. Another cue you'll learn more about in a later chapter is called anchoring. Anchoring allows you to carefully insert a cue in your session so your brain can automatically associate it with what normally follows. In this case, your association may lead to a deeper relaxation. Habits are all about associating cues and practicing something long enough for it to become automatic.

If it's possible to change habits in the brain, then you can change your suggestibility, even if you're struggling at first. Intentional actions bypass the default mode network, but your brain will always default back to what it knows best if you don't give it a consistent push. The human brain is a gorgeous, albeit insanely fragile, organ that needs to be encouraged to do new things with some effort, but the changes that can happen are phenomenal.

Chapter 5:

Beginner's Guide to Induction

How do stage performers and hypnotherapists induce someone? The same way they use hypnotic induction and state deepening, you can apply many of these methods to your self-hypnosis recordings. Self-induction undoubtedly takes practice, but that's part of perfecting your control over your mind. Not everyone responds the same way to each induction method, either. Some people respond better to verbal suggestions, and others respond well to physical gestures. Experiment with different induction methods and your hypnosis journey will become easier once you find the right one.

Induction Basics

Induction is the process of being guided into a more relaxing state where your mind is open to suggestions. Hypnotherapists use varying methods to induce a hypnotic state, and they can use state deepeners to increase your suggestibility before suggesting the changes you discussed with them. That way, they ensure you're sufficiently induced to produce the best results from your session. Chances are that you won't go too deep on the first session, but that's what your experimental visits are about. The deeper you go, the more likely you'll be to accept the suggestions. Please note that you'll still be fully aware of the session, and you'll most likely only experience posthypnotic amnesia if you trust the hypnotherapist to do so, or if you fall asleep. There's nothing wrong with falling asleep, even in a hypnotherapist's office. For them, your first visit is a learning curve, too. They also need to experiment with varying state deepeners before they find the one that works for you.

Additionally, a licensed hypnotherapist understands that the four models of learning can impact the way you respond to induction and deepening. Consider whether you learn better through reading, listening to a lecture, or getting physically involved in the action. This indicates what your learning modus is, and you can let your hypnotherapist know if you want them to have a greater chance of success the first time.

The four modes of learning that relate to hypnosis are verbal, non-verbal or kinesthetic, intraverbal, and extraverbal. If you learn easily through verbal communication, then conversational types of hypnotic induction work. If you learn easier through physically getting involved in projects, you'll do well with non-verbal hypnotic inductions where the hypnotherapist may tap your shoulder or touch you with permission. People who learn better with intraverbal suggestions are more likely to follow the tone of voice used during induction. Extraverbal learning is associated with your internal perception of meaning related to the words used.

Some hypnotherapists will use one type of induction suggestion, and others will use a combination of all four. If you're practicing self-hypnosis, you can cater to the four modes of learning because this allows you to turn your attention inward more easily. For example, as a verbal, intraverbal, or extraverbal learner, you can rely on your voice and chosen words in your recordings. As a non-verbal learner, you can add state deepeners that make you feel something, such as leveraging your arms or a rapid method like the shock inductions.

When visiting a hypnotherapist, know that three factors matter in your successful relationship. A good hypnotherapist needs rapport, intention, and prestige, which is something you should also consider when you're practicing self-hypnosis. The greater your relationship is with these three factors, the more successful you'll be. When entering a hypnotherapist's office, these three factors will determine whether you gel with them or not.

Rapport is something they build with you by recognizing your uniqueness. Think about it this way, you're more likely to open up to someone you feel comfortable with or know. Hypnotherapists should be able to chat with you to get to know you better before attempting induction. They need to boost your comfort levels, and they do it by using the valuable mirror neuron effect. Like sticks with like, so a hypnotherapist who mirrors your emotions and thoughts will likely work better than someone who sits with their arms crossed, waiting to induce someone they know nothing about. After all, you should have a chance to help your hypnotherapist understand what exactly it is you'd like to achieve in the sessions. Anyone who likes or values themselves will respond better to someone who seems similar to them. This isn't trickery; it's called rapport and a confident relationship. On the other hand, someone who isn't comfortable with themselves might also struggle with self-hypnosis. Be your authentic self while you attempt induction at home. Value your ambitions.

Intention is something that stems from the days of mesmerism, but it also matters in a successful visit with a hypnotherapist. Imagine walking into a hypnotherapist's office, and they give you this blank look. You want someone who will intend to achieve what you set out to achieve. Their intentions must be just as healthy as yours, and that applies to induction as well. You won't trust anyone who doesn't have the same intentions. Your intention with induction and state deepening is to reach a point where you can feel comfortable and open enough to actively and effectively listen to the suggestions laid out by the hypnotherapist. They should feel and show confidence while inducing you to the desired state. That way, your confidence will grow in them. You also need to intend your induction. The likelihood of your induction is based strongly on how much you and your hypnotherapist intend to produce it successfully. Focus all your attention on your will to make your effort successful, even in self-hypnosis.

Prestige is the final cornerstone of successful inductions at home or in your hypnotherapist's office. Are you likely to take medical advice from someone who never studied medicine? Are you prepared to receive tips from the cashier at Walmart before you build a new deck at home? Chances are that you'll always seek someone you know who has knowledge. How do you know they have knowledge? You know if they have prestige. Consider the reasons a stage hypnotist is so successful with inducing their audience and volunteers. Indeed, they can induce an entire audience if they have enough prestige. Their marketing has gained them a reputation for being known to induce anyone. A hypnotherapist places their certificates in the waiting room to show their patients they're reputable. We want advice and guidance from someone who knows what they're doing. They don't have to use fancy words to tell us what they know.

They merely have to display their prestige. That way, they become trusted. You don't want to be hypnotized by someone who claims to know how but has no social standing. Just the same, you also want to boost your confidence in yourself if you practice self-hypnosis. Own the knowledge you gain, and be confident that you can apply it as you learn more about hypnosis, suggestions, and inductions. You require self-prestige to make this wildly successful. If you don't believe you can induce yourself, you won't. This happens because you're adopting an inhibition that's mighty hard to break through. Do you think a hypnotherapist who claims to be new to the field will have a line of patients waiting at their door? No, they won't. You're learning about the science behind hypnosis, and you know what it does to the brain. Moreover, you'll learn about the myriad of induction techniques and state deepeners now.

Inducing and deepening your state is simple when you acknowledge your best mode of learning to create an easier response, and you can experiment with various methods to find your key to the world of hypnosis. You also know what to expect and encourage when you visit a hypnotherapist if you're still relying on them to grow more comfortable with yourself. Some hypnotherapists are so prestigious that you'll feel hypnotized when you walk into their office. If you gel this well with someone instantly, then you've found a great way to achieve those goals you desire. At the end of the day, inductions and state deepeners have the same desired outcome. Each one of them is a different path you can take to reach the same destination, which is an internal focus. Whether you're using a candle to induce yourself or a hypnotherapist is conversationally guiding you through visualization, you still want to reach that inner place where everything becomes clear and open to suggestions.

Rapid Inductions

Rapid inductions are used when time is limited and you want to deepen your state quickly before possibly applying additional state deepeners. Sometimes, they can take seconds. Some hypnotherapists use rapid inductions, which may be followed by a conversational piece before making the desired suggestions.

The first method is called a "shock induction." It sounds draconian, but it works. A hypnotherapist distracts you with something random before giving you a quick and not too painful shock. They'll also say 'sleep' or 'down' when the shock happens. This method kind of tricks the brain to go into deep relaxation. Remember that you're not sleeping. The word 'sleep' is merely associated with a deep state of relaxation. You'll notice some inductions use the word because our brains automatically associate it with the intended calmness needed in a hypnotic state. The word 'down' has a similar effect because you're associating it with going deeper. The brain prefers to follow the suggestion instead of trying to make sense of what happened, so induction is normally swift with this technique.

The second rapid technique is known as "pattern disruption." Our brains associate certain patterns in social situations, especially the subconscious mind. We tend to have an idea of what our interactions with another person will be like. We greet them, shake their hands, and then we have a set pattern that follows.

What happens when you disrupt the pattern? Quite simply, the subconscious mind gives up trying to make sense of the pattern disruption, and you fall into a hypnotic state. The pattern disruption induction happens when a hypnotherapist suddenly shakes your hand long after it was acceptable in your subconscious patterns. This confuses the subconscious mind, which then opens you up to a rapid hypnotic state. This disruption will accompany the words 'sleep' or 'down' again. As you'll notice, this induction also doubles as both a verbal and non-verbal suggestion.

The third rapid induction is called 'confusion.' It applies the same principles of the last induction method. The purpose is to confuse the brain so your focus has to increase while you fall into a hypnotic state. This induction method is used when a hypnotherapist overloads your brain with too much information, making it hard to focus on anything but the internal environment. For example, they may ask you to count backward from 500 in increments of 13 while you hold your arms out and focus on imagining buckets of water balancing on your arms. They may throw a whole bunch of instructions your way to make it impossible to focus. Humans and their brains are innately lazy in this sense, so the brain will likely enter a hypnotic state instantly when the hypnotherapist says the magic word 'sleep.' Resting and turning your focus inward is far easier than trying to pay attention to a list of ridiculous requests.

Another rapid technique is called "trust induction." Think of a time you went on a corporate or team-building excursion. Trust falls are a favorite practice in these excursions. Your hypnotherapist may use the same technique to induce you. This induction has the same effects as the shock induction. You may be asked to stand with your eyes closed while your hypnotherapist walks around you. At any random time, they'll ask you to fall backward while they catch you. As you fall into their arms, they'll say 'sleep' or 'down' again. This type of induction would require you to trust your hypnotherapist. Otherwise, you may not fall when they ask. The request will also come amidst a random conversation. You will and won't be expecting it at the same time, which also causes mental confusion.

An uncommon technique used by hypnotherapists to induce people rapidly is called "swish confusion." Indeed, it also creates confusion that exhausts the brain. A hypnotherapist may ask you rapid questions, such as "black or white," "cold or hot," and "summer or winter." The speed at which these questions are fired your way gives you hardly any chance to even think about the answers. Before you know it, the question will come that sends you into a hypnotic state. They'll suddenly ask "sleep or sleep" when you least expect it. You won't even have to answer as your mind will have one option: to go deeper into a relaxed state because the keyword 'sleep' was mentioned.

Rapid inductions aren't easy to apply in self-hypnosis. Hypnotizing yourself is easy once you understand the principles, but you won't be confusing or distracting your mind if you're doing this yourself. These techniques are favorites in hypnotherapy, and some stage performers use them to rapidly induce someone. For self-hypnosis inductions, you'll need to learn about many other types used by professionals.

Conversational Inductions

Almost all inductions are conversational to some extent, but some hypnotherapists are so good at what they do that they can hypnotize someone straight after walking through the door. The person also won't always be aware that the hypnotic session has started, but they'll start feeling relaxed immediately, which leads to hypnotic induction on its own in some cases. Highly suggestible people will be induced in conversational induction before they even realize what's happening. However, it remains a choice whether you go into the hypnotic state or not. If you're resistant, the hypnotherapist will use conversational induction to prepare you for deepening while you're talking about your plans or getting to know each other. Sometimes, hypnotherapists don't even use formal inductions if they apply the conversational part.

This works if the person being induced manages to reach a point of relaxation open to suggestion without deepening their state. Conversational induction may sound like a regular conversation between you and the hypnotherapist. The suggestions to induce you will be indirect and covertly hidden in the regular chat. It doesn't matter what you're talking about. The hypnotherapist may be telling you more about themselves while prepping you to talk about yourself. For example, they may use an introduction paragraph like this.

Thank you for seeing me on this *pleasant* day. I look forward to helping you find ways to *relax deeply* while we work toward finding your purpose for *hypnosis. Hypnotic effects* are *relaxing, calming,* and *overwhelming.* You may be one of my *many clients* who *falls deep into the hypnotic state. Going deeper is the goal,* and you may *feel your eyes grow tired.* You may *feel a sense of calmness overwhelm you* when you *choose to go deeper.* Many people find my *chair relaxing,* and it helps them *go deeper into the hypnotic state when they're ready.* You can *fall into a hypnotic state* whenever *you feel ready.* This is *all about you and your wish to fall into a hypnotic state.* You don't need to *imagine falling deeper* until you want to be *hypnotized.* We can chat for a few moments before *you fall into a hypnotic state.* It should be *a relaxing experience for you* where you feel naturally drawn to *go deeper.* Meanwhile, I'd like you to *start relaxing* and *choose when you'd like to fall into a hypnotic state.*

This introduction from a hypnotherapist may already have you hypnotized if you're highly suggestible. They carefully use priming words to establish your induction, even before you get into the session. The priming keywords in this introduction would be 'relaxing,' 'deeper,' 'calm,' 'hypnotic state,' 'when you're ready,' 'your eyes grow tired,' and 'overwhelming' to mention a few. Hypnotic induction keywords are a great way to relax someone before hypnosis or inducing them altogether. They can also work to increase your comfort with the hypnotherapist. This example even has a hypnotherapist building rapport with you. Additionally, these keywords can be applied to self-hypnosis recordings if you wish to relax for a few moments before falling into a deeper state. Think of any words that make you imagine relaxation, calmness, and hypnosis. You can even use the word 'sleep' because it simply represents the state you wish to achieve. Conversational induction is something most hypnotherapists will use to at least prime their patients.

Progressive Inductions

These types of inductions are great for any hypnosis practitioner who has time and wants to enjoy the full extent of the session. Whether you're recording your own sessions, or you're visiting a hypnotherapist, you'll likely experiment with one or more of these induction methods.

The "breathing induction" is one of the simplest methods. Deep breathing naturally calms you down and opens your mind to a deeper state. You can close your eyes or keep them open while every breath in and out has an intention. The breaths you take in will draw relaxation into your body and mind, and the breaths going out will slowly push out any resistance against a relaxed mind. A hypnotherapist may say, "Imagine yourself drawing calmness into yourself with each breath that goes deeper and deeper."

The "visualization induction" technique is a classic way of relaxing someone enough to make them suggestible. It can also work for regression therapy if you're going back to a memory to feel more confident or joyous. Nonetheless, the hypnotherapist might say, "Imagine yourself lying in the warmth of beach sand at your favorite, most relaxing destination." This form of induction is similar to guided meditation. Its main purpose is relaxation, and you can take yourself back to any place you enjoyed or even an imagined place in your recordings.

The "counting induction" is another popular choice, but it gets a better response from people with analytical minds. If you love numbers, counting backward while carefully curating each drop in depth can help you reach full induction. For example, a hypnotherapist may ask you to count down from 50 to one in single increments while repeating the words 'deeper' and 'calmer' interchangeably with each drop. As you drop from 50 to 49, you may go deeper. You feel calmer as you drop to 48, and you may go even deeper as you drop to 47. The countdown method is mainly a verbal induction though, so it might have to be combined with a progressive relaxation technique if you want better effects.

The "muscular relaxation induction" is when you scan your body to deepen your state of relaxation. A hypnotherapist may request that you focus on one area of your body while you allow the muscles to relax as you choose. They always start with one end of your body and work their way toward another end. They may say, "Allow yourself to feel your toes melting into a relaxed state while you may feel the need to go deeper down the rabbit hole." This is also a popular technique used in self-hypnosis.

The "tension-releasing induction" works similarly to the previous one. In this technique, a hypnotherapist will ask you to draw some tension into the muscle groups before releasing them. Slowly, you'll work your way through your body from one end to the other while they verbally guide your releasing efforts. They may say, "Pull your arm muscles tight from the hand to the shoulder while you hold it. Keep holding it. Hold it some more. Now, release the tension as you may feel the temptation to fall deeper into a relaxed state." This method also works well for self-hypnosis.

The "staircase induction" method must be one of the oldest progressive methods used by hypnotherapists and self-hypnosis practitioners alike. For this one to work, you need to visualize yourself taking steps down and down into a deeper space. Most people visualize a spiral staircase, and the length of it will depend on how deep you want to go. A tip with this method is to imagine yourself holding the rail to your left. This gives you an additional thing to focus on while you're imagining your feet leaving one step and touching another. The secret to making this work is that you must feel yourself falling into a deeper place. The feeling of falling into a deeper space should resemble that of the sensation you feel when an elevator moves down many floors.

You have to create this sensation of moving deeper and deeper down the staircase in your imagination. Some people use the elevator method, which applies the same rules. It takes some practice, but imagining the sensory experiences within this induction is what makes it more effective. This method doesn't even need verbal guidance, but you can add guidance to your recordings if you can't focus on your visualization. Hypnotherapists know how to verbally guide your journey down, including the sensory stimulation you need to experience.

Fixation Inductions

Fixating your attention to anything internal or external causes mental fatigue, which leads to hypnotic induction. Eye fixation and the fatigue that follows was first established by James Braid if you recall from Chapter 1. However, it was Milton Erickson who first recognized that someone could also be hypnotized by fixating their attention on imagined items (Mandel, 2019). In Erickson's experiments, he was able to hypnotize individuals by guiding their imagination verbally while their eyes were closed. He either gave them a real item in the direct environment to imagine once their eyes closed, or he simply directed their visualization with common imagined items. In one experiment, the individuals who imagined a metronome were induced even deeper than those who fixated on a real metronome. The point is that our brains become fatigued when we fixate our focus. It's a natural process, so these methods work for self-hypnosis and hypnotherapy sessions.

"Eye fixation" is the most commonly used induction in this category. Some people use candle flames, and others use a colorful pattern on a curtain. Any item can be used, but items that move can create faster fatigue. Candlelight can be observed as the flame dances back and forth. Subtly, your eyes are also following the rhythm of what you see. That's why metronomes and pocket watches were so popular in stage performances. The movement adds to the exhaustion of the participant's eyes when they have to focus on it. Naturally, once your eyes feel tired, you'll close them. If you're using a recording, you can cue this gradually for a minute or two before it happens. For example, you can say, "Your eyes feel heavier and heavier as the flame dances from side to side." The act of fixation alone can induce you, but adding verbal suggestions will double the effects. Most hypnotherapists will use a conversational induction tone while you fixate on the flame.

Your fixation also doesn't have to be visual. Indeed, you can visualize yourself focusing on this flame as it moves around. You can visualize a pocket watch if you want to try the stage approach. However, you can also fixate your attention on other sensations in your body. The "arm leverage induction" is another fixation method with a splash of progressive induction. You can either keep your eyes closed or open them as you stretch your arms out in front of you. Hold your palms down to the ground as you imagine buckets dangling from their ends. As you conversationally guide yourself into hypnotic induction in a recording, pay attention to how the buckets feel like they're filling with water. A hypnotherapist will keep reminding you how the buckets are growing heavier and heavier as more water pours into them. They'll encourage you to keep your arms stretched out, even if you're feeling tired. When they think you're ready to fall into a hypnotic trance, they tell you to drop your arms while saying "and down you go" or something similar. This induction method helps you fixate on the sensations in your arms.

The "spreading fixation" is the final method you'll learn about today. This one is complicated to practice at first, but it's a good induction nonetheless. You'll be required to rest your elbow on an armrest while you fixate your attention to the tips of your fingers. A hypnotherapist will keep your fixation here by tapping the tip of your middle finger. As your hold becomes tiring, you'll notice your fingers spreading slowly. Your attention must remain on the tip of your middle finger as the others spread further and further apart. You'll also notice that your hand starts moving closer and closer to your face. This is a natural magnetism caused by fatigue in your eyes and hand. A hypnotherapist will typically use conversational induction while your hand draws even nearer. As the tip of your middle finger touches your nose, they'll say 'sleep' or 'down.' This touch may also be followed by your eyes shutting. You can use this method in self-hypnosis if your recording paces it well.

Inducing yourself doesn't seem so complicated anymore, and you know what to expect if you visit a hypnotherapist now. Again, your suggestions will depend on your needs, but you can successfully induce hypnosis.

Chapter 6:

Hypnosis as a Therapeutic Practice

Hypnosis treatments have been investigated to see what this practice can be used for in clinical settings. Again, it can't be used to create outcomes beyond your biological or reasonable limitations. Hypnosis is not a miracle cure or some form of witchery. The heightened interest in its application among various mental and physical conditions proves that hypnosis can change your life for the better, but don't expect what can't happen. Your motivation and intention are too precious regarding successful practice to believe fake stories. Disappointment will only turn the practice into a worthless failure. Our expectations set our outcomes, responses to the results, and how we succeed in getting there.

Basic Improvements

The most basic improvements you'll see from hypnosis are increased awareness, focus, and relaxation. These are three skills we underestimate. The world has certainly gone insane, and we can easily get lost in the overwhelming need to enter the race. We don't know how to stop, relax, and focus on our personal goals anymore. First, we need to be aware of where we are now and where we intend to be. Second, we require focus to maintain our trajectory toward our goals. Finally, we also need moments to collect ourselves, and that only happens in relaxation. Constantly aiming for your goals is a valuable skill, but successful people will tell you that you need time to recover from the race now and then. Not taking breaks from the madness will only push you right to the brink of insanity yourself. At one point in history, we always had to be on our toes. We needed to chase the holy grail for survival, but that's changed now.

We are no longer racing toward our goals because we have wild animals on our tails. We aren't being chased by something that threatens our lives. Well, one can consider financial obligations and family responsibilities as factors that could encourage us to pursue our goals with grit and boundless energy, but they don't threaten our safety as humans. We feel motivated by our families because we love them. We feel motivated to pursue our financial and career goals because we don't want to get into trouble. However, we get swept up in this race, always trying to reach our goals, but we end up losing track of where we were going in the first place. The failure to stop and notice the journey itself can cause us to lose focus on our goals. Moreover, we aren't even aware that we lost track of our goals until we mentally break down. In simple terms, hypnosis teaches you to relax, be aware of your internal environment, and focus on what matters.

Hypnosis improves your awareness because you travel inward to see what your mind desires and needs. Practicing this heightened state of awareness also improves the benefits outside of sessions. Your focus might not be perfect at first, but you'll get there. It's no wonder our focus is so poor when we're surrounded by electronics and social media constantly nudging our attention. We've forgotten how to focus on one thing, and hypnosis trains your mind to sharpen the attention you need in and out of sessions. Remember that consistent practice turns into habits. At some point, your subconscious mind and the default mode network in your brain will automatically make decisions and pay attention to what matters, even in the external environment. Most importantly, hypnosis teaches you how to relax again. A busy mind that can't switch off is a sign of poor attention and awareness, but relaxation helps you practice improvements in both. Besides, you also need some downtime once in a while.

Mental Health Potentials

Hypnotherapy is being used widely as a complementary treatment initiative in many health conditions. The reason for this is that it's proving to be effective. In some cases, hypnotherapy is a valuable tool in targeting symptoms of other conditions, but it can also be applied successfully to improving your mental well-being. Mental health problems start in the brain, and that's where hypnosis targets phenomenal changes to help you lead a better life. Some areas of mental health and its relationship with hypnosis have been researched, and the results were in favor of using the practice.

One study led by the University of Helsinki in Finland examined how hypnotherapy benefited adults who suffered from attention deficit hyperactivity disorder or ADHD (Virta et al., 2015). This condition is the definition of lacking attention, making this a perfect study. People with ADHD have impulsive and hyperactive tendencies, but their biggest challenge is sitting still or focusing on a single task for long. The study included 27 ADHD patients and 31 regular people in a control group. Both groups were measured for suggestibility, and they were given a three-minute task called a continuous performance test (CPT). The CPT was an auditory test, and it was administered four times each before hypnosis, during induction, while the participants were hypnotized, and after they were brought out of hypnosis. Both groups showed a slight decrease in reaction times on the second and third rounds of CPT tests during induction and hypnosis.

The ADHD group further showed decreased reactions in the final CPT after hypnosis while the control group showed an increase again. The study concluded that hypnosis can reduce reaction times, which shows an increase in selective attention in ADHD individuals. The control group returned to their normal attention and reaction responses after the session, but the ADHD group maintained their decreased reactions for longer. The decreases also showed less activity in the basal ganglia, amygdala, and temporoparietal lobes, which are part of the default mode network. Increased activity was seen in the executive control network required for higher attention. This is great news because slowing down the reaction times for ADHD adults proves that we can decrease impulsivity so they can focus on completing tasks. Hypnosis may help people with ADHD lead more fulfilling lives.

Other mental health improvements from hypnosis include the reduction of symptoms in dementia patients. Forensic psychologist Simon Duff at the University of Liverpool studied his dementia patients over nine months (University of Liverpool, 2008). Duff and his associate Dan Nightingale divided the patients into three groups. The first group received mainstream medication and treatment for their condition while the second group was required to attend weekly group therapy sessions. Current affairs and news were discussed in the group therapy. The final group was allocated to hypnotherapy sessions weekly.

The group on mainstream treatment showed a decline in their condition after nine months, and the group therapy participants showed no improvement or decline. However, the hypnosis group showed promising improvements in various skills. Relaxation, motivation, concentration, a willingness to socialize, and a better quality of life were unfolding among the hypnosis patients. Duff was so impressed that the University of Liverpool now offers special hypnosis treatments for dementia patients. Further research is still required to see whether the same results can be seen in longer studies or where patients' cognitive abilities have declined a lot.

Hypnotherapy is being used more widely since the explosion of research has proven so successful in various health conditions. A comprehensive review of hypnotherapy and mental health was published by the American Psychological Association (Smith, 2011). Hypnotherapy proves to be a valuable tool in complementing treatments like cognitive-behavioral therapy (CBT). The review shows that it helps in cases of post-traumatic stress disorder (PTSD), acute stress, chronic stress, depression, burnout, and anxiety. It can also be used to overcome phobias and undesirable habits, which are both related to mental health conditions. The success of hypnotherapy as a complementary or direct approach in mental health can lead to various improvements. It can gradually expose someone to things they fear to reduce anxiety, and it can help people take control of obsessive tendencies.

Controlling your mind can do wonderful things. People can focus on stressful situations better after hypnosis, and their emotions don't fluctuate, which means their stress response is under control. A person's ability to detach themselves from undesirable habits like smoking and drinking is increased after hypnotherapy, albeit it's not successful in all cessation cases. It works for some people and not others. The research showed that hypnotherapy is as successful in smoking cessation as other therapeutic and medical cessation methods. It does increase your chance of quitting, but it may rely on your individual experience with hypnosis. You'll have a greater chance of success if rapport with a hypnotherapist is established first. The success rate of self-hypnosis is dependent on the magnitude of your intentions and your dedication to quit. Although, we've already established that these are necessary traits for successful hypnosis.

People also adopt a more positive perspective, which also decreases anxiety and depression. Sometimes, our mental state is so badly influenced by the affairs of the world that we succumb to depression and anxiety. Hypnotherapy helps us regain control over the way we respond to the world. We can't change what's happening in the world, but we can change how we react to it. Hypnotherapy has also successfully managed to increase people's self-control, and it made waves in changing the burnout situations we often end up in. Burnout is a terrible result of the madness and busyness of the world, but taking better control of your mind, thoughts, emotions, and habits can reduce burnout as a bonus. As soon as your mind is more peaceful, you find the time to juggle everything. Additionally, you also find the time to take care of yourself. The more you take care of yourself, the further negative emotions, thoughts, and burnout reduce so you can cope with the world again.

Hypnotherapy may not be a cure-all for mental health conditions, but it's the universities dropping the ball on training programs that concerns the APA. Hypnotherapy has proven to be effective in many studies, so the APA believes it can be a valuable psychotherapy tool. Many universities are providing courses now, but self-hypnosis may be the answer to the gap if you can't find someone with rapport and prestige. This is particularly a difficult time that will go down in history. You can either be the person who mentally breaks under the weight of a world changing to something we can't even recognize, or you can be the person who flourishes and maintains your mental well-being. Hypnotherapy and self-hypnosis can help you achieve this. It gives you more tools to cope with life.

Physical Health Opportunities

Hypnotherapy continues to show great improvements in many conditions, especially as a complementary therapy offered when patients suffer from chronic pain or undesirable symptoms. Many of our symptoms can be worsened or reduced if our brains choose to. A review of the benefits of hypnosis was conducted by the Mayo Clinic and published in *Mayo Clinic Proceedings* (Stewart, 2005). According to the review, the first successful establishment of hypnotherapy in clinical trials for two years was hosted by the Council on Mental Health. It was after this that the American Medical Association (AMA) approved it as a credible approach in contemporary medicine in 1958. The AMA even pushed for training centers in America so that the skill can be used and applied by numerous therapists. However, the review also shows a myriad of other conditions that were treated successfully with hypnotherapy.

Dermatological studies were included in the review. Hypnotherapy was used in a study originally published in *The Lancet* (Sinclair-Gieben & Chalmers, 1959). The patients underwent hypnotherapy as a complementary treatment for warts. Ten patients were part of the trial, and one of them was highly suggestible to hypnosis. The other nine patients were moderately suggestible. The highly suggestible patient's warts disappeared after only six weeks of added hypnotherapy treatment, and the moderately suggestible group's warts disappeared after three months. Hypnotherapy was used to avoid pain and scarring, as well as the side effects of anesthetics during the procedures used to remove warts. In normal cases, warts usually return as the human papillomavirus (HPV) tends to stay in the system for two years. That's why warts can be hard to get rid of. Also, during this time, wart removal wasn't as simple as today. Other than wart treatments, hypnotherapy was also successful in dermatitis and psoriasis.

Some studies also looked at gastrointestinal disorders. Irritable bowel syndrome (IBS) is the most commonly studied disorder in this spectrum when it comes to hypnosis. One study in England divided 30 patients with severe IBS into two groups (Whorwell et al., 1984). Both groups were consuming placebo drugs for the condition. Placebo drugs are used in trials where the participants are told the drug is real but it's not. It's a mental trick commonly used to help patients believe that they're receiving treatment, which is sometimes enough to make them feel better. Anyway, participants in one group were receiving regular psychotherapy while the other group indulged in seven hypnotherapy sessions. The results were undoubtedly different. The hypnosis group showed significant positive changes in bowel habits, and they had reduced pain and symptoms. The psychotherapy group didn't show much difference after the trial.

Another way hypnosis can help you physically is during childbirth. A study was conducted at the Aberdale District Maternity Unit in Wales (Jenkins & Pritchard, 1993). Pregnant women were approached at antenatal classes to ask whether they wanted to try hypnotherapy by having six sessions before they gave birth. A total of 126 women giving birth for the first time were grouped against a control group of the same factors. Another 136 women giving birth for the second time were also grouped against a control group of the same factors.

The length of the first and second stages of labor during normal childbirth was measured in all four groups during labor. The average time for the first stage of labor in the firstborn groups was 6.4 hours for hypnosis moms and 9.3 hours for control moms.

The second stage of labor for firstborn moms lasted 37 minutes for hypnosis moms and 50 minutes for control moms. The average time for second-time moms in the first stage of labor was 5.3 hours for hypnosis moms and 6.2 hours for control moms. The second stage of labor in the second-time mom groups was 24 minutes for hypnosis moms and 22 minutes for control moms. The first- and second-time hypnosis moms also reported less discomfort during both stages of labor. Hypnotherapy can decrease the length and discomfort of labor for first- and second-time moms. Anyone who gave birth before will know that these results are good enough to encourage hypnosis during pregnancy.

Another study published in *Pediatrics* looked at the relationship between chemotherapy side effects and hypnosis (Zeltzer et al., 1991). Chemotherapy is notorious for leaving patients with severe nausea and vomiting. Three groups of 54 children undergoing chemotherapy were used in the study. The first group received hypnotherapy to help with their chemotherapy distress, pain, nausea, and vomiting. The second group received CBT relaxation exercises, and the third group only received placebo treatments. Each child's anticipation of nausea and vomiting was also recorded before the chemo sessions. The children in the CBT relaxation group maintained their anticipatory and post-chemo symptoms, meaning they didn't worsen or improve. The placebo group of children showed worsening anticipation and symptoms after chemo. The hypnosis group of children showed the most positive results. Their anticipation of nausea and vomiting decreased before chemo, and their symptoms didn't flair as much after chemo. Hypnosis proved a win here again.

Chronic pain is another condition hypnosis can help with. A study of 40 patients with refractory fibromyalgia was published in *Rheumatology* (Haanen et al., 1991). Fibromyalgia is a condition that causes moderate to severe chronic pain and fatigue. Pain and hypnosis research is abundant, but this study shows how it can help for chronic conditions as the patients had this condition for over eight years. The patients were either given hypnotherapy or physical therapy, and they had to follow up after 12 and 24 weeks. The hypnotherapy group showed significant improvements in their ability to manage their chronic pain, and they had better energy levels in the mornings at both follow-ups. Chronic pain is just another issue you can manage with hypnosis.

Using hypnotherapy during dental and surgical procedures goes back a long way as you learned in Chapter 2, and hypnosis continues to help patients deal with surgery. Hypnosis is also more commonly used as anesthesia today. Research published in *Minerva Anestesiologica* confirmed that hypnotherapy can successfully be used in the place of anesthesia if the patient is willing and suggestible (Facco, 2016). In fact, it can be used as the only anesthesia in minor surgery, dental procedures, and invasive procedures on selective patients. It should be recommended as an option before surgery. Hypnosis can also be used as an adjunctive option with anesthesia, or it can be used before and after surgery to reduce recovery times. It's an attractive technique used previously by surgeons in the Second World War before amputating a soldier's legs. However, it should only be administered to someone who requests it in surgery.

Hypnotherapy has many applications in contemporary medicine if you return to the review from the Mayo Clinic. It can help you lose weight, complement pulmonary treatments, and even manage headaches. What you use hypnosis for is still your choice, but many different benefits can be produced, physically and mentally.

Chapter 7:

Neuro-Linguistic Programming (NLP)

Neuro-linguistic programming is a technique often confused with hypnosis. NLP is a different technique, and it's much younger than the traditional concept of hypnosis. It's commonly used among life coaches who wish to help their clients achieve greater results in their lives, albeit some hypnotherapists use methods similar to NLP coaches, and others apply some NLP techniques like anchoring and mirroring in regular hypnotherapy. See it this way: NLP, hypnosis, and even mindfulness can overlap, especially as we learn to perfect all the techniques available in our modern society. Learn what NLP is and how it can benefit your journey so you can decide whether it's an option for you.

NLP Explained

The origins of NLP sound strange if you consider what the co-founders called their first books. Richard Bandler and John Grinder chose to name their books *The Structure of Magic* volumes one and two. Don't be fooled by the name though. Richard Bandler was a 20-year-old psychology student at the University of California in the early 1970s when he befriended doctor John Grinder. Bandler first studied computer sciences and mathematics, but he soon changed his major to behavioral sciences. Grinder was an associate linguistics professor at the university. The two men were intrigued by the work of psychotherapist Virginia Satir who developed gestalt therapy, which is a mindfulness-based therapy that focuses on a unique person's present challenges and experiences. Everyone has varying life experiences, and it makes sense not to treat all patients the same.

Bandler began hosting workshops where gestalt therapy was used. Satir's therapy was interesting for another reason. Grinder leaned toward what made the therapy work, which, in his mind, was linguistics. Both men realized the therapy worked because the therapist was using a certain language to communicate with each individual patient. They studied the reasons for Satir's exceptional excellence with recordings and her written work. The key factor was her language choices, which weren't quite the same as hypnosis. Satir was able to influence her patients positively because she structured her language with them based on how their brains understood it. Bandler and Grinder began assessing other effective communicators to see whether they also influenced their clients or patients. They even studied Milton Erickson's work so they could design a new technique that uses conversational style hypnotic effects.

Just as hypnosis was seen as a quack practice in its earlier days, NLP was treated the same way when it started. Hypnosis has the advantage of numerous scientific studies backing it over a long period, whereas NLP doesn't have that benefit yet. Some studies have proven that NLP works, but the studies are still limited. The reason NLP is hard to study is that it's also hard to define. Since Bandler and Grinder's work developed into something that could be used in corporate, psychological, and personal fields, it has exploded into a fast-moving evolution. In simple terms, NLP is the study of how our minds design a map based on our experiences, biases, inhibitions, goals, and motivations, and all this is processed in what NLP coaches call a language. Every person's language is perfectly unique. The way your brain processes information is influenced by your map, which is different from everyone else's. In psychology terms, this is called perception.

The reason NLP focuses on the language of the brain is that the map can only be interacted with if it understands the language received, which may be verbal, kinesthetic, or through any of the five senses. Verbal languages are the most commonly used to interact with the brain on a level it will understand.

However, NLP coaches often spend months or years perfecting their ability to speak directly to all our consciousnesses, and they may or may not use an induction technique similar to hypnosis to broaden our awareness in each conscious mind. For NLP coaches or practitioners, language is the key. Consider this: neuro means brain, linguistics means language, and programming means change. NLP is not hypnotherapy in any way, but it's considered by some people to be similar. It's a more modern way of interacting with your map or perceptions so you can learn to accept where you are now before making your desired changes.

That's how mindfulness is added to the mix. Using NLP to understand your neurological map before attempting to change it is a mindful practice. Mindfulness encourages us to see ourselves for who and what we are in the present moment without judging ourselves harshly to establish what our maps look like first. We have to accept who we are before we can change anything. We have to know how our thoughts are formed and how our patterns are embedded. Once we recognize our true selves, we can work on improving our creativity, work performance, mental health, and happiness. NLP also detects the inhibitions and self-limiting beliefs in our minds so we can find ways to work forward and change them. Our biases exist deep within the subconscious mind, and they largely impact our automatic behaviors. In many cases, people don't realize what their biases are until they investigate them.

Your neurological map and biases are designed through lifelong conditioning. Every experience you live through with your senses collects data for the brain to add to this map. For example, your teacher always said you'll never amount to anything, and you tend to repeat this negative bias daily with self-talk. You tell yourself that you'll never succeed. You think you'll never be more than you are now. Even thoughts create pathways on this map because every thought ignites a chemical reaction. Hence, your map is designed by internal and external experiences, which happen from your earliest days. Having no confidence in yourself is a bias that NLP would surface from your subconscious mind. This bias influences every decision you make, so it has to be gradually replaced after accepting that it exists. The reasons it exists may also be exposed. Anyway, NLP coaches are trained to encourage the brain to recognize this bias.

You can become an NLP practitioner yourself, but experience matters in this field because it also relies on rapport and experimentation. Some coaches are well-seasoned, and they'll pick up your language cues in one session. They'll understand your problems and needs before you even mention them simply by listening to the language coming out of the map. NLP works through consciously using language to bring about changes in someone's map, which impacts their behavior and thoughts after each coaching session. It also takes time like hypnosis does. Those biases are ingrained into your map, so you need to work slowly on removing them. A coach will first build rapport before they gather information from what you say and *how* you say it. Then, they'll help you work toward goals that will benefit your personal ambitions. They also can't make you do anything you don't want to, just like hypnotherapists.

One simple change you could experience might just be the most profound of them all. According to research published in *Counseling and Psychotherapy Research*, NLP has successfully helped 106 patients with personality disorders (Stipancic et al., 2010). People with personality disorders have altered perceptions of the world, meaning their maps are more biased than most people. The patients in the study showed improved perception, leaning toward positive map building. They also had more positive outlooks on life, improving their quality of life. The study concluded that NLP is as effective as CBT. Again, this is a small-scale study, but it proves the one thing NLP coaches attempt to do, which is to change the map inside the brain because it represents the perceptions we have of the world. Some NLP coaches also encourage hypnotherapy because the two techniques can complement each other well.

What was first called magic as a poor choice of title for a book is a credible and official practice used by countless coaches around the world today. Improving the way you see life, and learning to overcome the biases and inhibitions that hold you back, boosts your mental health as well. Additionally, some people may respond so well to NLP that they can go on to influence other people. Their positive and success-driven attitude becomes their new language, which tends to rub off on others.

What to Expect

NLP is not something you can easily apply to your self-hypnosis recordings. It takes practice and training, but that doesn't mean you can't delve into the working of the technique to start using it eventually. However, what you can expect from an NLP coach will consist of basic principles first. NLP coaches believe that we're in a natural hypnotic state most of the time, but we aren't in control of it unless we take charge. Coaches are also ambiguous, meaning they structure your journey through your map without actually filling out the content. For example, they might say, "You may choose the option that feels right for you and makes you happy." They won't likely imprint answers on you for their benefits, such as saying, "You will apply for the promotion at work on Monday at 10." Ambiguity is common among NLP coaches, which is great because it gives you the freedom to choose what you want to change.

A coach also uses tonality and pacing to lead you through the session, whether you enter a hypnotic state or not. Some people won't enter the deepest state of relaxation or the hypnotic state. A coach may also presuppose hypnotic states if they don't think you're open to your subconscious mind. If they see your eyes getting droopy, they may say, "That's right" or "It's good to feel relaxed now." The coach may also shock you by interrupting your thought patterns during the session so they can lead you back toward what you're trying to achieve. Your benefits are the only goal for an NLP coach. Coaches also use a technique called 'utilization' if something interrupts their lead. Maybe someone honks their horn outside, interrupting your train of thought. Quickly, the coach will utilize this sound by saying, "You may notice the person honking in the distance, and you may feel like the sound is moving further and further away now."

Ultimately, your coach will attempt to get you relaxed enough to follow their lead while the content of the session will remain ambiguous. Well, unless you've asked them to help you with something specific. This is what you can expect from your coach in terms of the entire process. The language used by them will also be broken into four parts. The human brain recognizes four language patterns. Let's say your coach is using a hypnotic trance to open your subconscious mind. The patterns they use in all their verbal and non-verbal communication will be commands, embedded commands, linkage phrases, and process language. Commands are self-explanatory. Your coach will subtly encourage certain commands, such as "you may feel deeply relaxed now." Where hypnosis uses suggestions, NLP uses ambiguous commands, which seem closer to indirect suggestions.

Embedded commands are a way for NLP coaches to carefully reinforce the command until the desired hypnotic state is achieved. They try to avoid using the word 'or' as one example. Imagine asking a client if they'd like to relax or calm down. This only causes confusion, which isn't encouraged during NLP. Coaches embed the commands by using words like 'and,' 'when,' 'because,' and 'as though.' They'd say, "You may start feeling relaxed and calm as though you're drifting into a deeper space because when this happens, you become deeply and completely relaxed." This sentence alone embeds the command five times. The coach may also lower their voice with each embedding, and they may use hand gestures to emphasize the commands if you're a kinesthetic learner. You may even notice how they try to bring deeper meaning to the embedded command, and any gestures will do the same.

Packing commands like "start now," "relax deeply," and "feel good" in-between embedded commands can also help the brain accept them without thinking too logically. Your conscious mind remains awake, just like traditional hypnosis, but you don't want the default mode network interfering with the commands by erecting walls. For example, they might say, "You may start now and feel good because when you enjoy this feeling of relaxation, you'll be more open to the opportunities and possibilities." Four embedded commands surround four regular commands in this sentence. They might also start sentences with embedded commands to reinforce them further. For example, they may say, "And as though you're drifting into a calm place and feel deeply relaxed, you may feel good when you enjoy the calmness and serenity of this space." Five embedded commands surround four commands in this sentence.

The word 'now' is also a powerful amplifier at the end of sentences again. A coach may place it anywhere. They also know how to start sentences that set the pace for embedded and regular commands. Some set-up sentence starters include "luckily, you can," "when you," "if you were to," and "a person can." Let's turn this into another sentence you may hear by staring and ending it with embedded commands. "If you were to relax and feel good as though you're engulfed in calmness and serenity when you sit gently in that chair, you may feel a sinking depth reaching out as though you're about to fall deeper and deeper now." This sentence has six embedded and regular commands each. The way your coach speaks to you is all about the science of language they've been trained to use. The most important part of this effective communication to open your conscious minds is to use commands and embedded commands.

The linkage language used by coaches is similar to an embedded command. It's any word they use to associate one idea with another, such as the word 'and.' Coaches will often link three factual commands before subtly using an ambiguous command. For example, they might say, "You're listening to the sound of my voice and sinking into the chair, and you want to relax, and you may start relaxing now." The first three linked statements are factual while the fourth one is a command. The word 'and' works as a simple linkage between them, even though the sentence sounds grammatically overwhelming. Hypnotic suggestions also don't always make sense. However, you won't notice these strange links once your subconscious mind opens up. Your conscious mind stays awake, but it's not flagging the illogical sentence structures. Even something as simple as sentence structures may put up walls if you don't allow the conscious mind to rest and watch without interference.

Process language is the last of the four patterns you'll notice in a session. The coach uses their ambiguity to design a structure where you can move in any direction on the map you choose. They'll make suggestions, and they'll attempt to lead you to something that benefits your session, but you're ultimately in charge of how you want your brain to process the language. Maybe you discussed your poor mental health with the coach before the session. They gathered information from you so they can direct you toward a place on your map where you may find answers. Using all three other patterns, they'll help guide your brain to understand the language. They might embed commands that make you think more about the changes you want when you're at home again. Changing your mind and removing biases don't happen instantly, so leaving your mind willing to process the language further outside the session can help you gain more clarity.

The coach may also embed careful directional commands so you don't react to situations the same way when faced with similar challenges outside of the session. A coach may leave you with a processing language by saying, "When you notice other people using patterns you wish to have, and you notice how much they may benefit you, you may also copy their patterns now." This is how a coach may leave your language processing in a condition where it can continue learning after the official sessions. People who learn to control their maps, especially those who have ambiguous coaches, can continue to learn patterns from other people's maps they find interesting or desirable.

These are the basics of what you can expect in a session with an NLP coach or trainer. Your state will always depend on how deep you're willing to go, even though the coach is embedding stronger reinforcement in each sentence. Words we believe are redundant in regular communication can help you effectively interact with your map.

Favorite Techniques

Some techniques are commonly used by NLP coaches. Some of them are used at the beginning of your relationship, and others are used after your coach understands your ambitions better. Discuss the various techniques with a coach so they can also understand your needs better. Here are some of the techniques to which you may be introduced.

The "mirroring technique" is used by many NLP coaches to build rapport with their clients first by making use of those mirror neurons again. Your brain's map is likely to open up and accept the directional cues from someone who mirrors your language, verbal and non-verbal. You have to learn to trust yourself and the coach, so coaches must apply the mirror technique first. You may notice your coach reflecting what you say, or they may smile when you do. Most of the mirrored responses will be too subtle to notice if your coach is well-trained. This technique may help you feel relaxed more easily, making your mind's map think it's opening to someone just like you. Just go with it. You'll feel supported in an environment you can accept better. Feeling comfortable will help you explore the necessary emotions and thoughts. Your coach will also find it easier to lead and pace your conversations.

The "reframing technique" is used to help clients replace negative statements and invisible words with new thought patterns. For example, maybe you approach an NLP coach to help you fight depressing thoughts and emotions. You tell them, "I don't want to feel depressed anymore." Nothing seems wrong with this statement, except that the word 'don't' isn't registered by the subconscious mind. This statement is negative and has the opposite effect on your goals. The coach will slowly introduce you to new ways of talking to and thinking about yourself. They might teach you to say, "I'd like to start feeling happier each day." Similar to how negative tones and language can cause problems in traditional hypnosis, it can also give the subconscious mind the wrong ideas in NLP. A coach will know how to help you start changing negative emotions caused by these thoughts to more optimistic outcomes. This technique can be used to increase or decrease specific emotions in clients.

The "belief changing technique" targets self-limiting beliefs that became habitual. Perhaps you always say you're terrible at dancing or you can't escape from depression. These are self-limiting beliefs, and they come from elsewhere. They've been installed in your mind with a lifetime of experiences that made you think this way. People who believe they can't do something will never do it. These beliefs are destructive in every way. The coach will identify what your self-limiting beliefs are and help you change them to your advantage. They'll encourage you to explore the reasons for these beliefs, and this journey may just help you see who they belong to.

You'll be able to understand what your current state of mind is when you think this way, and you'll recognize how these assumptions bring you zero benefits, which must happen before you change them. The coach merely leads you through the directional aspects you need for self-exploration. You do the rest. Coaches may use presuppositions to lead you, such as "this map is not my territory" and "if someone else can do it, I can learn to do it." The first presupposition is simply reminding you that your map's experiences were guided by other people's interactions throughout your life, and the second one reminds you that you can mirror the maps of others if you choose to.

The "anchoring technique" is a method we've discussed before. It wasn't traditionally used in hypnosis, but NLP has introduced modern hypnosis to anchors. A coach will gently guide you to feel something you desire, such as happiness or confidence. Once you experience an emotion, the coach will gently command that you anchor the feeling you're experiencing with a physical cue. Sometimes, they can take you back to a time you experienced the emotion, or they can guide you to it with visualization. The anchor can be as simple as tapping against your knee or rubbing your index finger against your thumb. This associates the action with the feeling, and you'll be able to access the feeling by repeating the action outside of sessions. If anchors are placed correctly, the attached emotions can be accessed anywhere, any time.

The "creative visualization technique" is used to carry someone into a mindfulness-based visualization where they can revisit a time they experienced joy or confidence. The same technique can be used to explore the future to remove self-limiting beliefs and biases. It can be used to question habits as well. Many coaches use this method to guide clients to a place of self-acceptance, which is necessary to understand what the map looks like first. Once you can see your map, you can communicate effectively what you want to change.

The "storytelling technique" is similar to the last one, but it encourages a client to turn something pressing into a story so they can reach the desired end in a visualization. Coaches should only direct clients in this technique, even if they know what's bothering them.

You must be able to see the steps that need to be taken because it's all for your benefit. For example, you're using this technique to play out the end when you're stressed about a presentation at work. The coach may carefully guide you to source the inhibitions standing in your way before directing you to tell the story as though everything works out perfectly. You'll be allowed to design the entire story in your mind, and some clients even say it out loud as the coach guides them. The purpose is to end the story on a high note, which often gives you ideas of how you can overcome challenges. Sometimes, we feel like we'll fail only because our minds are too noisy to think of the steps needed to succeed.

Opting for NLP is a great way to give yourself a modern kickstart on your hypnosis journey. Some hypnotherapists use this modern technique alongside their hypnosis practice. You know what you can expect now, and you know why it works. Everyone's perception is different, and their maps are just as unique. Getting straight to your mental map could open a world of opportunities for you.

Chapter 8:

Other Modern Methods of Hypnosis

NLP is not the only modern form of hypnosis you can apply to your life to establish desirable changes. Hypnotherapy has evolved, and knowing the many ways you can enjoy hypnosis in the modern world only gives you plenty of reasons to try it. Today, some self-hypnosis practitioners are developing their own styles simply by learning about the ones available. The most valuable secret of hypnosis is that it can be individualized and curated to fit your needs. The best way to start is with a hypnotherapist, but there are many ways to make hypnosis work for you. Other than NLP, you have five main modern styles of hypnosis from which to choose.

Suggestion Hypnosis

Suggestion hypnosis is the most direct and traditional form of hypnotherapy. It's also called direct suggestion hypnosis. It's the easiest type of hypnosis to start with and understand. This is the kind of hypnotherapy most people would expect. The hypnotherapist may spend a few moments getting to know you and what your needs are for the session before diving right in. Some hypnotherapists won't always get to know you or your needs well before starting the session, which is the reason many seasoned practitioners avoid the type. However, it's a great start for new hypnosis practitioners who want to get the feel of things. If you notice your hypnotherapist isn't bothering with gathering information before applying direct suggestions, you can either look for someone else or make it known that you wish to be more involved in the process. Traditional hypnotherapy doesn't always allow patients too much involvement in the suggestions, which are the commands being communicated to our open minds.

Request that you work with your hypnotherapist to craft the suggestions before induction. It's hard to think any of them will deny this if you mention it. Maybe you just want the hypnotherapist to help you solve a problem like smoking or a lack of confidence. Remember to consider your hypnotherapist's prestige, and if that's good to go, you can trust their ability to help you quit smoking or become more confident.

After all, you may not construct every detail of the suggestions, but licensed hypnotherapists with high prestige will likely know what will work for you. Suggestions you may hear from this type of hypnotherapist would sound like this.

"You're starting to feel relaxed as the chair wraps itself around you."

"You feel yourself falling deeper into a depth previously unexplored."

"Notice how you're sinking deeper and deeper as my words guide your journey into the depths of comfort and relaxation."

As you'll notice, they won't use the words 'may' or 'can' because they're outright directing you. You'll still have some form of control over your induction and deepening, but their words won't ask if you're ready to slip into a deeper state. It will just be applied. You may or may not slip deeper when they use direct suggestions. Just because they're instructing you to do something doesn't mean you will. Once induced, you may hear suggestions like this.

"You no longer feel the need to buy another pack of cigarettes."

"You want to breathe healthily while you cycle and swim."

"You feel the overwhelming sensation of confidence flooding over your body in this relaxing state."

The second suggestion implies that the patient wants to breathe better while cycling and swimming. This is great if the person partakes in those sports. If the patient hasn't indicated that they live an active life but struggle with breathing, then the session might not be so effective. The last suggestion also vaguely speaks of confidence flooding through the patient. It doesn't remind them of a time they experienced such confidence, and it specifically tells them how to feel confident but in a vague situation. If the patient discussed this with the hypnotherapist, then they might have suggested that the person remember a time of absolute confidence, or they might've asked them to imagine themselves feeling confident with a task specified before the session.

Suggestion hypnosis works wonderfully, but you must make sure you're setting the right pace with your hypnotherapist. You want them to use suggestions unique to you so they break through the inhibitions and biases.

Regression Hypnotherapy

Would you believe that you can change your memories? Truthfully, we can never change what happened to us, but we can rewrite the way we remember it. Regression hypnotherapy does just that. Some people call them false memories, but the success of regression types of therapy has allowed people to recover from trauma.

According to research conducted by New York University, memories can be changed as long as it happens soon after they were retrieved (Sample, 2009). The window of success was proven to be within three minutes and six hours after someone retrieves the painful memory. This means you have plenty of time during hypnosis to regress to something that caused pain so that you can rewrite it with new knowledge and even false memories if that helps you cope better. Memories can never truly be trusted as any police officer will confirm. As soon as we access it, it becomes warped and small details change. Each time we access it, the memory changes more and more.

The fact that regression therapies work so well could also be to blame for hypnotherapy not being used in courtrooms. People won't likely remember the precise details of what happened every time they retrieve a memory, even without intervention to change the memory. However, this makes regression hypnotherapy a valuable tool against overwhelming anxiety, PTSD, and phobias, especially if you're entering hypnosis to alter the memory with new knowledge. Regression is a way to focus on the core of any problem, which is the memory itself. This type of hypnotherapy doesn't focus on the symptoms that appear from the memory. In fact, most hypnotic techniques focus on problems and not the superficial symptoms they create. In regression hypnotherapy, you'll be taken back to the core memory that caused you pain or other psychological symptoms. Your hypnotherapist will then help you introduce new information that may have changed the memory if you knew it then.

Let's say you're experiencing psychological symptoms after being in a car crash. The memory is painful for you because you were the driver. Three people got hurt, including you. This memory alone has so many psychological effects. You don't trust yourself as a driver anymore. You don't want others in the car with you. You also blame yourself for hurting everyone in the car because you think you're responsible for what happened, even if the facts report otherwise. The main reason this memory makes you blame yourself is that you chose to leave the movie before enjoying another iced coffee. That coffee would've changed the outcome because you wouldn't have been in the line of that speeding car that never stopped at a traffic light.

It's easy to see how someone could hold this against themselves because they think their decision is what caused the accident. A regression hypnotherapist might approach this scenario by returning you to the moment you and your friends walked out of the movies. The knowledge you have now is that you might've missed the accident if you had a cup of iced coffee first. In the new memory the hypnotherapist guides you through, you'll be encouraged to make a different decision, knowing what you know now. This in no way confirms that you were to blame, either. However, it allows you to remove the one factor you blame yourself for. The hypnotherapist will run you through a false memory where you spend extra time at the theatre, and you all get home safely. In a case like this, someone needs to adopt a false memory, especially when no one else agrees with the way the person blames themselves. What about the friend who spent five minutes in the bathroom? What about the other friend who chatted on the phone for another two minutes?

Everyone's decisions led to the same outcome, so no one, in particular, is to blame for what happened. Every decision we make changes the next minute of our lives. What if the speeding car chose to have an iced coffee instead? None of it would've happened then. Life is not about fate and destiny; it's about how each tiny decision everyone makes can change what comes next.

Regression hypnotherapy can help someone like this who blames themselves as though they were the only person who made a decision that night. Regression hypnosis will help you relive past experiences with a new knowledge toolkit or even just knowing what you know now. If you feel like you have some memories that cause psychological symptoms or hold you back from pursuing something you want, you might consider regression hypnotherapy. This example was extreme, but the same hypnosis can be used for phobias.

Let's say you're afraid of enclosed spaces, which is called claustrophobia. Maybe your phobia caused a bit of an embarrassing situation at work. The power went out, and you were stuck inside an elevator with colleagues for five minutes. In that time, you completely lost it. The things you said, and the way you behaved made a total fool of you in your mind, and now you can't face your colleagues. The knowledge you have now is that you weren't stuck in a situation for hours or days. It only lasted five minutes. The hypnotherapist can regress you back to being stuck in the elevator, but this time, you know it will end soon, so you don't behave the way you did the first time. Calmly, you count down the five minutes with your eyes closed. Subtly, the hypnotherapist is also giving you coping tools for when it happens again. Closing your eyes and counting your breaths is a coping mechanism.

It doesn't matter what memory you need to retrieve; a hypnotherapist who specializes in regression hypnosis can help you retrieve and modify it so that it can't cause symptoms anymore. Regression therapy can also be practiced in your self-hypnosis recordings. However, make sure the recordings are positive and lead to the right outcome. Your memories are too fragile, so you don't want to accidentally make them worse. If you can relax deeply, and you have great control during your recorded sessions, you can attempt regression hypnosis. Otherwise, seek a professional hypnotherapist.

Primers

Primers are used by people learning to practice hypnotherapy at home if they don't feel comfortable visiting a professional, or they don't have enough experience for self-hypnosis and self-recorded sessions yet. Self-hypnosis practitioners eventually move away from primers as they learn to customize their own sessions that work for specific goals. For new practitioners, there's an ocean of options available online and on paid apps so you can become familiar with the process. A primer will induce you into a hypnotic state, and you'll make positive changes to your life, depending on your ambitions with hypnosis. The only setback with primers is that you can only use them for specific outcomes. Some primers might be used to suggest changes in your work performance, and others may suggest that you feel better about your body image. There's a primer available for nearly everything if you look hard enough.

Not being able to modify them is what doesn't always work for everyone. Even the induction used during the primer may not be the best one to relax you. We all respond differently to varying words, tones, and paces. A hypnotherapist attempts to customize their approach to you in person, but a primer is a pre-recorded session that doesn't cater to varying modes of learning or preferred suggestions. You may not respond as well to "feel yourself folding deeper into yourself" as you do to "feel the chair engulfing your body and taking your mind to a deeper plain." Suggestions are the lifeline of any type of hypnosis, you won't be experiencing the full benefits of the session if the inflexible kinds don't speak to you. On the other hand, highly suggestible people are likely to respond to most sessions as long as they choose one that fits their desires. Keep in mind that you can become more suggestible, but you need a few practice rounds first.

If you choose to use primers, don't give up right away. Find a session that aligns with your goals, such as smoking cessation, confidence building, or optimism boosters. Listen to it a few times before deciding that it doesn't work for you. Your intention also matters, so intend to make it work. Be open to the suggestions, and if you feel no different after a few sessions, look for another primer with a different voice, tone, and choice of words. The point is that some primers may or may not work for you, but give them a chance before moving on to another one. Primers allow people to use professional-style hypnosis sessions without a clinical hypnotherapist being present, so you have to apply them with your mind set on success. Just like you realize a certain hypnotherapist isn't your best bet, you'll recognize with time that some primers don't work effectively for you. As long as you listen to them with the full intention of experiencing some relaxed state and improvements, you'll be fine.

Ericksonian Hypnotherapy

Erickson's type of hypnotherapy is a popular choice because it's indirect. This style is considered to be the opposite of traditional hypnosis. Milton Erickson was the first man who allowed patients to have greater control over whether they became relaxed or not. They had more control over whether they accepted the suggestions or not when he used indirect and permissive styles of guiding his patients. That's how the

Ericksonian hypnosis method was born. Patients have a choice when visiting a professional who offers this type of hypnosis. The session may be conversational, including the induction. However, you'll never be hypnotized against your will. Professionals will speak to you first while they gently encourage your openness to the coming induction. The permissive style of this hypnosis allows patients to enter a hypnotic state only when they're ready.

If you don't like being directly suggested to relax and calm down, then this style is a much smoother option for you. Indirect suggestions use words like 'can,' 'may,' 'when,' and 'if.' For example, your hypnotherapist will focus on inducing you or making suggestions by saying something like this:

"If you're feeling the urge to fall into a deep relaxation, and you want to open your mind to the possibilities, you may start feeling relaxed more deeply now."

"When you're ready to go a little deeper, and when you feel a calmness coming into your mind, you can enter the relaxing state that beckons you."

The entire session will be permissive. You'll have choices whether you want to go deeper or not. You have choices in any type of hypnosis, but Ericksonian hypnosis reminds you that it's a choice with every suggestion. Even before you enter the session, the hypnotherapist will explain what to expect in the same permissive tone. Ericksonian hypnotherapists may also use the conversational primer induction to get you relaxed and build rapport before making any formal suggestions. As you learned in Chapter 5, the conversation you have from the first moment may already be priming you for better induction, but the permissive style of this hypnosis type won't allow the hypnotherapist to induce you without your permission. Once induced, you'll also be given permissive suggestions. Here are some examples of what might be suggested, depending on your goals.

"You may choose to do what's right in this situation, and you may decide when to do it."

"When you walk into the room, and you see the other person waiting, you may choose to walk over to them with your shoulders straight."

"If you're in this situation again, and when you remember the options you now have, you can make the best decision for you."

These are simple and vague examples of what you'll hear in your suggestions from the hypnotherapist. They'll direct you to what they think can benefit you, but they'll only permit you to take action. You can choose to take action or not. A traditional hypnotherapist will directly suggest that you take action, but you would better be able to choose whether or not you do it in Ericksonian hypnosis. Both types of hypnosis still require you to control what comes next, but this style of hypnosis plants permissive and unspecific seeds from which you can grow thoughts and ideas. The traditional hypnotherapist will plant a seed with more specific ideas that can grow, whereas an

Ericksonian hypnotherapist will plant vaguer seeds with options so you can perceive it in a way that benefits you better. This style of hypnosis is widely popular today.

Self-Hypnosis

What may be the most modern form of hypnosis is self-hypnosis. Although self-hypnosis can be as flexible as your imagination allows, it can also be the most complicated one to master. Even seasoned hypnosis practitioners constantly improve or alter their self-hypnosis journey, and many of them don't come right until they've ingrained their self-confidence and experience. The reason self-hypnosis is a complicated journey is that you have to play the role of a hypnotist and the one being hypnotized at the same time. That's why many practitioners use pre-recorded sessions so they can separate the two entities. The brain gets confused unless you separate them. The positive side of self-hypnosis is that it provides a wider range of benefits because you can customize it to any problem you encounter in life.

A self-improving and self-healing strategy that changes as your life experiences change is the greatest way you can stay on top of things. Take someone who suffered from insomnia their whole lives. They spend six to eight weeks sleep training themselves with self-hypnosis, and to their surprise, they don't seem to be bothered by sleep problems anymore. It's incredible to sleep like a normal person after years of having insomnia. However, this problem no longer needs addressing because the brain has trained itself now. The practitioner will seek out a new goal to change something else in their lives. Perhaps something new comes along. Their work has always been received as excellent standards, but the company they work for is expecting changes to their rhythm now, making them uncomfortable. New employees came along, and they set a trend of excellence this person can't seem to match.

We should never compare ourselves to other people, but we should prepare ourselves for changes because it's the only thing certain in life. What may be excellent today is outdated tomorrow, so this person can structure new recorded sessions, which may not be perfect at first. You'll notice that using your own recordings can be ineffective as you experiment with various state deepeners, anchors, and suggestions. That's okay. Don't beat yourself up for not succeeding the first time. Self-hypnosis means you can always change your recordings to improve their effectiveness. For the working example, this person recognizes the problem. Their feelings of becoming obsolete are impacting their motivation at work, which only makes them present poorer quality results. They can't hypnotize themselves to be better than the new employees, but they can encourage motivation to improve and stand out by using the right suggestions.

Your recordings will likely change as often as the weather, and that's a good thing. You need to find suggestions and inductions that work for you. Self-hypnosis is not a self-destruct button, so you can't implode if you use the wrong suggestions. Obviously, you're not going to suggest negative things because this results in unwanted consequences. However, you're going to choose the suggestions that speak directly to you. You must build rapport with yourself but know when a session sounds wrong. Recognize when a session just isn't doing it for you, and record another one. Listen to primers, visit a hypnotherapist, and gain some experience to grow your confidence. You can also find words that resonate better with you by closing your eyes and saying them in your mind. Repeat words commonly used in hypnosis sessions, such as 'deep,' 'sleep,' 'relax,' and 'calm.'

How do you feel as you say the word 'deep?' This tells you how your mind responds to the word. If you feel your mind moving down one notch when you think about it, you've found a working suggestion. How do you feel when you hear the word 'relax?' If you feel any part of your body releasing in the slightest when you hear it, you've found another working word. You can sit in a quiet place and experiment with how different words make you feel before attempting your first recording. Play around with various induction types to see if your mind responds before adding the suggestions to a recording. Can you imagine yourself feeling that sensation of dropping lower and lower if you see your feet descending steps behind closed eyes? Can you feel the heaviness of your arms if you hold them out straight in front of you?

Fortunately, our phones allow us to record multiple sessions, so we can record many attempts before we perfect them. The secret to starting a self-hypnosis habit is to first learn how to relax deeply. If you find the words and imagined factors that help you reach the hypnotic state, you've already won half the battle. The suggestions you insert after your induction are reliant on what you need to change, so no one can tell you what to say. Another piece of great advice is to record your sessions in parts. Some people become so well-seasoned with their practice that they can separate themselves as a hypnotist easily, and it can happen during recordings. After all, you have to use your hypnosis voice and tone, so it can affect you. Writing your scripts before recording them can help you stay out of hypnosis during recordings. Once you start recording, break the script down into four sections, and spend time doing something else between the sections.

The final advice for self-hypnosis is that you need to remember to end the session. Hypnotherapists end sessions by saying, "and now you'll be awake and fully alert." Again, you were never asleep, but your brain needs to be reminded that you're back from the hypnotic state. Choose a simple reminder for the end of your recordings, which will become crucial as you grow your suggestibility.

Deciding which type of hypnosis is right for you is a matter of trying them all. You can even try multiple types at once. Stacking them can help you target changes from various angles. Otherwise, you can stick to suggestion hypnosis if you want a direct approach.

Go with Ericksonian hypnosis if you want a permissive type, but attempt self-hypnosis as early as possible. You can also let your hypnotherapist know you're open to learning self-hypnosis. They may give you some pointers and help you design a structure and suggestions from a professional perspective. Hypnosis is not a one-shoe-fits-all approach. Everyone benefits from various types. The more you experiment, the closer you come to realizing which type or collection of techniques benefits your life the most.

Conclusion

Hypnosis seems like a strange phenomenon to some people, and that's what creates so much confusion. People think about the stage performers who hypnotize people to do ridiculous things in front of large audiences, or they watch a movie where the writers clearly didn't understand hypnosis. Sometimes, the misinformation can even lead to failed attempts when you want to practice hypnosis. Failure is not what it seems, and that's part of the mystery behind hypnosis. Maybe you want to learn more about what science has to say about this technique. Perhaps you find it interesting after hearing about the benefits someone else enjoyed. The beauty with hypnosis is that there's a technique for everyone, new and seasoned, even if the person has perceivably failed with it before.

Hypnosis can easily become a magical phenomenon when you're reading unreliable sources, especially when they all oppose each other. This is when you have to rely on the facts. You can't expect to learn about something from people who don't even practice it. You have to learn how to master skills from people who've been trained to teach you. They must have experience, and that often requires them to test various options. Through experimentation, many misconceptions are already laid to rest because of the one golden rule in hypnosis. Just because a technique works wonderfully for one person doesn't mean it will benefit another person. Good hypnotherapists know this, and that's why they care to take time and learn to know you and your needs.

Anyone can claim to be a master persuader, but not everyone can apply the three essential tools to make most people comfortable. The uniqueness of every modern version of hypnosis, and the personalization of the approach itself, may just be the answer to someone's question about why they failed. Everyone's suggestible to some extent, and we can all find a method that speaks directly to our most relaxed and hypnotic mind. We also won't all feel the same under hypnosis.

Let's compare hypnosis to fishing or any common hobby, lifestyle, or habit. Does everyone love fishing? No, not everyone does. Do they all fish the same way? No, there are many different types of fishing today. Can everyone sit for hours watching a bobble in the water? This is the part that overlaps hypnosis. If the motivation is right, anyone will watch that bobble for hours or even days.

If there was no food left in this world, and the only way we could eat was to fish, we'd all find a unique way to do it, and we'd persevere through the parts we don't like. Maybe we don't love fishing, but we love eating fresh fish, and we know the benefits can't be denied, so we find ways to improve the one factor we dislike: fishing itself. That way, we take something that didn't seem to work in our favor, and we turn it into something that does. Hypnosis is similar. We may not all respond the same way, and it may not feel as exciting to everyone, but we all benefit once we figure out how to deal with the fishing stage. Let's say the fishing stage is the experimentation part of your journey, and the fish you need for nourishment is the myriad of benefits you can enjoy after perfecting your fishing style.

You can also choose not to benefit, but you wouldn't be interested in learning more if you didn't want to take charge of your mind. Some people just want to learn how to better face a problem with a few hypnotherapy sessions, and they'd love to know more about the mysteries behind it. However, others want to dive deep into the science behind hypnosis so they can use it for ever-changing improvements in their lives. Some people may survive a while on one fish, but most people will hunger for more if the practice works for them. Either way, you know what the history of hypnosis is now. You also know the surprising methods used to inspire modern hypnosis, and you know the famous names associated with it in science and psychology fields. You even know what happens in the brain, which explains how the hypnotic state impacts you.

You're also well-aware of the many fish you can collect with ongoing practice, and you have a few secrets to make your scripts, suggestions, influence, and inductions better. Who knew a simple thing like mirroring another person can have such profound effects? The brain remains a masterpiece, but it can be your masterpiece if you grab the reins. You can paint the picture of what you want your brain to remember, think, feel, and act out. People who don't choose to practice hypnosis are missing the most damaging secret. Their minds are still processing information, whether they control it or not. Anyway, you also have the six most popularly practiced modern hypnosis techniques now, and you know what to expect from each of them. Maybe you want to dabble in NLP, or perhaps suggestion hypnosis is the one that sounds best for you.

Remember to try different methods, and no rule says you can't use multiple methods to learn and gain experience before you master your own techniques at home. Self-hypnosis is only complicated if you don't know how to prepare for it, but you have many tips to grow your personal practice now. The hundreds of people I've helped on this journey also required some guidance and experience before they could master self-hypnosis, but many of them did it. The others chose to use different methods, working with myself and other seasoned practitioners. Some of the people I helped also turned to professional services by hypnotherapists, and that still makes me proud of them.

It doesn't matter how they managed to master their minds; they still found a way and never quit until they did. There's no greater feeling than being in charge of your thoughts, emotions, and behaviors. Opportunities flourish in people who actively choose to control their outcomes as much as humanly possible. I hope the mysteries unveiled in this book will help you take charge of your mind. You can always let me know by leaving a comment or review. Sharing our experiences with others is what makes this journey even more exhilarating. My wish for you is that you find the mastery you're capable of finding. Don't allow misinformation to cloud your judgment again. Go out there and become the fullest version of yourself.

References

APA. (2021). *Hypnosis*. American Psychological Association. https://www.apa.org/topics/hypnosis

Bach, B. (2016, July 28). *Stanford study shows what happens in the brain during hypnosis*. Scope; Stanford Medicine. https://scopeblog.stanford.edu/2016/07/28/stanford-study-shows-what-happens-in-brain-during-hypnosis/

Beale, M. (2021b). *NLP hypnosis and meditation*. NLP Techniques. https://www.nlp-techniques.org/what-is-nlp/hypnotic-influence/

Brooks, S. (2019, April 4). *31 hypnosis techniques (the most comprehensive list)*. British Hypnosis Research. https://britishhypnosisresearch.com/hypnosis-techniques/

Emamzadeh, A. (2021, February 2). *21 myths about hypnosis*. Psychology Today. https://www.psychologytoday.com/us/blog/finding-new-home/202102/21-myths-about-hypnosis

Facco, E. (2016). Hypnosis and anesthesia: Back to the future. *Minerva Anestesiologica*, *82*(12), 1343–1356.
https://pubmed.ncbi.nlm.nih.gov/27575449/

Fritscher, L., & Block, D. B. (2019). *Conquering phobias through hypnotherapy*. Verywell Mind. https://www.verywellmind.com/hypnotherapy-2671993

Fulcher, R. Z. (n.d.). *What is a hypnotic induction? How do you hypnotise someone?* HypnoTC. https://hypnotc.com/what-is-a-hypnotic-induction/

Gardner, B., & Rebar, A. L. (2019). *Habit formation and behavior change*. Oxford Research Encyclopedia of Psychology. https://doi.org/10.1093/acrefore/9780190236557.013.129

Gravitz, M. A. (1988). Early uses of hypnosis as surgical anesthesia. *American Journal of Clinical Hypnosis*, *30*(3), 201–208. https://doi.org/10.1080/00029157.1988.10402733

Haanen, H. C., Hoenderdos, H. T., van Romunde, L. K., Hop, W. C., Mallee, C., Terwiel, J. P., & Hekster, G. B. (1991). Controlled trial of hypnotherapy in the treatment of refractory fibromyalgia. *The Journal of Rheumatology*, *18*(1),

72–75. https://pubmed.ncbi.nlm.nih.gov/2023202/

Hammer, A. G. (2019). *Hypnosis | definition, history, techniques, & facts*. Encyclopædia Britannica. https://www.britannica.com/science/hypnosis

Handel, S. (2009, June 29). *Hypnosis explained (debunking the myths)*. The Emotion Machine. https://www.theemotionmachine.com/hypnosis-explained-debunking-the-myths/

Hypnosis Motivation Institute. (n.d.-a). *Ancient hypnosis - hypnosis in history*. Hypnosis. https://hypnosis.edu/history/ancient-hypnosis

Hypnosis Motivation Institute. (n.d.-b). *Hypnosis in the modern era - hypnosis in history*. Hypnosis Motivation Institute. https://hypnosis.edu/history/hypnosis-in-the-modern-era

Hypnosis Motivation Institute. (n.d.-c). *The fall of animal magnetism - hypnosis in history*. Hypnosis Motivation Institute. https://hypnosis.edu/history/the-fall-of-animal-magnetism

Hypnosis Training Academy. (2014, October 20). *How to fine-tune your hypnotic voice*. Hypnosis Training Academy. https://hypnosistrainingacademy.com/hypnotic-voice/

Jansen, C. (2019, March 5). *Hypnosis for anxiety and depression.* Resources to Recover. https://www.rtor.org/2019/03/05/hypnotherapy-in-mental-health/

Jenkins, M. W., & Pritchard, M. H. (1993). Hypnosis: Practical applications and theoretical considerations in normal labour. *BJOG: An International Journal of Obstetrics and Gynaecology, 100*(3), 221–226. https://doi.org/10.1111/j.1471-0528.1993.tb15234.x

Kandola, A., & Legg, T. J. (2017, December 20). *Neuro-linguistic programming (NLP): Does it work?* Medical News Today. https://www.medicalnewstoday.com/articles/320368

Kirsch, I. (1997). Suggestibility or hypnosis: What do our scales really measure? *International Journal of Clinical and Experimental Hypnosis, 45*(3), 212–225. https://doi.org/10.1080/00207149708416124

Krippner, S., Adkhani, K., & Viggiano, D. (2019, December 10). Shamanic healing ceremonies, hypnosis and the survival of the suggestibles. *Online Journal of Complementary & Alternative Medicine.* https://irispublishers.com/ojcam/fulltext/shamanic-healing-ceremonies-hypnosis-and-the-survival-of-the-suggestibles.ID.000554.php

Lynn, S. J., Gautam, A., Ellenberg, S., & Lilienfeld, S. O. (2018). Hypnosis: Science, pseudoscience, and nonsense. *Pseudoscience.* https://doi.org/10.7551/mitpress/9780262037426.003.0015

Mandel, M. (2019, March 4). *The ultimate guide to hypnotic inductions.* Mike Mandel Hypnosis. https://mikemandelhypnosis.com/hypnosis-training/hypnotic-inductions-ultimate-guide/

Mongiovi, J. (n.d.). *Phenomena of hypnosis.* John Mongiovi. http://johnmongiovi.com/phenomena-of-hypnosis

Mongiovi, J. (2017, January 26). *The practice of retrospection.* John Mongiovi. http://johnmongiovi.com/blog/2017/01/26/retrospection

NLP Techniques. (2018). *100+ NLP techniques list. top NLP techniques.* NLP Techniques. https://www.nlp-techniques.org/what-is-nlp/nlp-techniques-list/

Ponton, L. (2016, May 17). *All about hypnosis and hypnotherapy.* Psych Central. https://psychcentral.com/lib/all-about-hypnosis-and-hypnotherapy#2

Primed Mind. (2021, February 23). *Types of hypnosis & hypnotherapy techniques.* Primed Mind. https://primedmind.com/types-of-hypnosis/

Ramanathan, R. (2020, January 16). *5 neuro-linguistic programming (NLP) techniques for coaching*. Coach Arya. https://coacharya.com/blog/neuro-linguistic-programming-nlp-techniques-benefit-coaching/

Reeves, D. (n.d.). *Hypnosis in ancient civilizations*. Ecstatic Trance Postures. https://www.cuyamungueinstitute.com/articles-and-news/hypnosis-in-ancient-civilizations/

Rizzolatti, G., & Craighero, L. (2004). The mirror-neuron system. *Annual Review of Neuroscience*, *27*(1), 169–192. https://doi.org/10.1146/annurev.neuro.27.070203.144230

Robertson, D. (2019, July 25). *Beginners guide to the history of hypnosis (timeline)*. The UK College of Hypnosis and Hypnotherapy. https://www.ukhypnosis.com/2019/07/25/beginners-guide-to-the-history-of-hypnosis-timeline/

Sample, I. (2009, December 9). *Memories can be "rewritten" to make them less traumatic*. The Guardian. https://www.theguardian.com/science/2009/dec/09/memories-rewritten-anxiety-disorders

Sinclair-Gieben, A. H. C., & Chalmers, D. (1959). Evaluation of treatment of warts by hypnosis. *The Lancet*, *274*(7101), 480–482.

https://doi.org/10.1016/s0140-6736(59)90605-1

Smith, B. L. (2011, January). *Hypnosis today*. American Psychological Association. https://www.apa.org/monitor/2011/01/hypnosis

Stewart, J. H. (2005). Hypnosis in contemporary medicine. *Mayo Clinic Proceedings*, *80*(4), 511–524. https://doi.org/10.4065/80.4.511

Stipancic, M., Renner, W., Schütz, P., & Dond, R. (2010). Effects of neuro-linguistic psychotherapy on psychological difficulties and perceived quality of life. *Counselling and Psychotherapy Research*, *10*(1), 39–49. https://doi.org/10.1080/14733140903225240

University of Liverpool. (2008). *Hypnosis shown to reduce symptoms of dementia*. Science Daily. https://www.sciencedaily.com/releases/2008/07/080728111402.htm

Virta, M., Hiltunen, S., Mattsson, M., & Kallio, S. (2015). The impact of hypnotic suggestions on reaction times in continuous performance test in adults with ADHD and healthy controls. *Plos One*, *10*(5), e0126497. https://doi.org/10.1371/journal.pone.0126497

Whorwell, P. J., Prior, A., & Faragher, E. B. (1984). Controlled trial of hypnotherapy in the treatment of severe refractory irritable bowel syndrome. *The Lancet*, *324*(8414), 1232–1234. https://doi.org/10.1016/s0140-6736(84)92793-4

Young, G. (2019, August 15). *What happened when Freud found hypnosis*. Institute of Applied Psychology. https://iap.edu.au/when-freud-found-hypnosis/#

Zeltzer, L. K., Dolgin, M. J., LeBaron, S., & LeBaron, C. (1991). A randomized, controlled study of behavioral intervention for chemotherapy distress in children with cancer. *Pediatrics*, *88*(1), 34–42. https://pediatrics.aappublications.org/content/88/1/34.short

Zur Institute. (2020). *Clinical hypnosis: Myths, realities and science*. Zur Institute. https://www.zurinstitute.com/clinical-updates/hypnosis-clinical/

www.ingramcontent.com/pod-product-compliance
Lightning Source LLC
Chambersburg PA
CBHW020256030426
42336CB00010B/796